# Act Like a Business
# Think Like a Customer

# Act Like a Business
# Think Like a Customer

MANAGING YOUR BUSINESS USING
LOYALTY, RELATIONSHIPS, AND ENGAGEMENT

## DR. ELIJAH G. CLARK

FIRST EDITION

Designed by E.C. & Associates

Act Like a Business. Think Like a Customer
Visit website at www.ActLikeABusiness.com

Printed in the United States of America

ISBN: 1548048275

ISBN-13: 978-1548048273

*To my valued client partners*
*and the E.C. & Associates team*

# CONTENTS

# Act Like a Business
# Think Like a Customer

# INTRODUCTION

Do customers *really* need your product or service? Of course not. But, there are some customers who actually do want what your product or service offers. The reality is that customers are solicited by plenty of businesses, and they have more options than they can count when it comes to purchasing a product or service. There is rarely anything special about one product over another. That leaves the questions: How are you any different from the rest? What makes *you* so special? If your ideal customer had 10 options in front of them, why would they select you over the competition?

Most customers have been so beaten down by poor quality businesses and individuals that they would much rather watch a do-it-yourself YouTube video, Google a solution, or get advice from friends and family on social media.

If you want customers to choose your business, you must give them *more* than a "solution" that they can get from anywhere. Of course, customers do want you to give them a solution, but more than anything, they want to like you, which is much more important than your solution or reputation. To impress your customers or prospects, you have to satisfy their needs and desires while also connecting with them emotionally. To grow your business, you can't just treat a customer as one of many, but treat them as a unique individual. With a growing society of independent customers, if you don't show your value in the form of a good personal relationship, your business will likely fail to grow loyal followers.

As humans, we are greatly influenced by our relationships. We enjoy being members of loyalty programs and networking groups that align with our goals. We patronize certain supermarkets, gas stations, and banks, and make most of our purchases from select companies. This showing of consumer loyalty is due to an unspoken relationship that exists between us and the businesses and brands we support. These brands make us happy, we like them, we trust them, and their consistency is calming in a chaotic world of too many choices.

Relationships are natural, and our preference for who we develop relationships with are often based on our past experiences and expectations. Similar to dating, customer relationships involve courting and evolution into a mutually satisfied connection or a breakup.

As a business owner, you have to successfully develop good relationships with your customers, and not be just another option. If you haven't had a referral in a while, you may not be pleasing your customers as well as you think. It's possible that you may have great services; your networking game may be strong and attracting plenty of prospects; but if your customers aren't consistently purchasing or coming back, you need to figure out what's going wrong, and you need to fix it.

If you're a professional — whether an entrepreneur or an executive — you need proven, high-level strategies to really make your business grow, and it all starts with understanding the needs of your customers. To sustain a relationship with a customer, you've got to think like a customer. Every time you visit, call, or send an invoice to your customer, consciously or unconsciously, your customers are asking themselves questions like: *Why did I hire this company or purchase this product? Do I still need them? Is this worth what I'm paying? Am I making progress? Am I seeing the results they promised? Is this the best company to purchase from?*

You must make it a priority to hear your customers' wants and concerns. Focus on what they like, want more of, and what they want less of.

In this book, I cover topics that will help you strengthen your business and develop successful business and marketing strategies to enhance your sales and productivity. My goal is to help you get your business to where you want it and to show you that it can happen without digging into your profits.

Most customers – the ones you want – look at your product or service as an investment. Then there are those customers who simply want to buy a product at the lowest possible cost. Through this book, I hope to help clarify how you can attract the right customer and make the OVERALL value of your business the focus of your customers, and not just your prices. It's time that you concentrate your efforts on having high-quality customers and high-ticket sales.

Let's start with Chapter 1.

# CHAPTER 1

## What Customers Want

## LOYALTY AND RELATIONSHIPS

As humans, we are greatly influenced by our relationships. We enjoy being members of loyalty programs and networking groups that align with our goals. We patronize certain supermarkets, gas stations, and banks, and make most of our purchases from select companies. This showing of consumer loyalty is due to an unspoken relationship that exists between us and the businesses and brands we support. They make us happy, we trust them, and their consistency is calming in a chaotic world with an overwhelming amount of choices.

Relationships are natural, and our preference for who we develop relationships with are often based on past experiences and expectations. Similar to dating, customer relationships involve courting and evolution into permanency or a breakup. At some point in every relationship, there is the question of whether the relationship has a future. At that moment of questioning, the relationship either continues down a happy road, or it ends.

**The Courting.** In relationships, everything starts perfectly. You show the prospect your best self as the ideal candidate for a long and fruitful relationship. The seduction begins. Promises are made, benefits explained, enticements for loyalty are offered, and declarations are made as to how you and they can create magic together. They find you to be a worthy partner and the two of you begin a wonderful journey.

**The Breakup.** As the months go by, they start to feel unhappy that you aren't paying much attention to them. You forgot their birthday and the last time you were together you were caught flirting with another prospect. They stop answering your calls and the last time they visited something just felt different. Eventually, they start complaining about small things and indirectly question what you are doing with their money. You see it in their behavior that the relationship is coming to an end.

The reality is that the relationship was over a long time before it ended because of those small things that you did or didn't do which got you to this point. It could have been something as simple as not responding fast enough to their email or text, not paying attention to their needs and wants, or that you've failed to notice and respond to how they've changed as a person. Either way, they are no longer attracted to you, and they no longer believe in your optimism about the future.

To sustain a relationship with a customer, you've got to think like a customer. With every visit, call, or each time you send an invoice to your customer, consciously or unconsciously, your customers are asking themselves questions such as; *why did I hire these guys or purchase this product? Do I still need them? Is this worth what I'm paying? Am I making progress? Am I seeing the results they promised? Is this the best company to purchase from?* Remember, it's usually many little things that add up to their decision to terminate the relationship. If you are aware and address those issues from the start, and keep focused on satisfying the customer throughout the relationship, you're in a much better position to sustain the relationship.

## RELATIONSHIP BENEFITS

Building relationships with your customers is a must when looking to start and grow your business. Some of the substantial benefits of building a quality relationship with customers are explained below.

**Customer Satisfaction**: Customer satisfaction is an important measurement of how a product or service meets or surpasses the customer's needs. It is a reliable indication of the potential for repeat business and brand loyalty. Customer satisfaction can be attained only if your customer has an overall good relationship with your business and you consistently meet or exceed their expectations. In today's competitive marketplace, customer satisfaction is an important performance factor and a basic differentiator of business strategies. Hence, the more satisfied the customer, the stronger the bond they have with your business.

**Customer Retention**: Customer retention is a strategic process to keep or retain your existing customers and deter them from using other suppliers or organizations. This is only possible when there is a quality relationship between your business and the customer. Usually, a customer will remain loyal to a particular brand or product as their needs grow and only if those needs are properly fulfilled.

**Referrals**: The most cost effective approach to grow your customer base is through referrals. When customers feel satisfied, they are encouraged to become brand advocates for your business.

These referrals are beneficial for your business considering there is little to no cost associated with this process. Referrals are an optimal form of marketing and profit generation.

**Revenue Growth**: When your business maintains a healthy relationship with customers, revenue will always increase considering current happy customers tend to purchase more. There is also the potential for a satisfied customer to purchase additional products or services when offered the option to bundle those products and services. For instance, if a satisfied loyal customer has home insurance from an insurance company that they trust, there is a high probability that the customer will also purchase property and auto insurance from that same company.

**Retention Cost**: The cost to service existing satisfied customers is substantially less expensive than that of acquiring new customers considering there is no acquisition cost, your business should already know the needs and wants of existing customers, and active customers will have fewer queries and complaints as they are already aware of your business's processes, products, and checkout flow.

## COMMON INTEREST

In a relationship, it's important that you have common interests. It's hard to keep a relationship moving forward if you have nothing or little in common. Factors that customers consider when entering a relationship with your business include the business's reputation, niche, work ethics, communication, customer service, and if your business has the resources to meet their needs.

Customers select you for a reason. In the initial meeting with your customers, you should try to determine that reason by simply asking, "What is it that you want from me or my business in this relationship?" or "Why did you decide to meet with me today?" Additionally, ask yourself what you want from your customers and always outline that during the meeting. Don't just focus on the product or service benefits that you offer, but also outline your unique processes in achieving results.

**Terms of Agreement.** Once you decide on how the relationship should move forward, write it down and make it clear. Just because you understand your terms, does not mean that your customer has a clear understanding. If you are selling a product on a website or through a physical location, you should have important terms mentioned multiple times during the course of business, in contracts, and on your website. Furthermore, educate your customers to prevent confusion about the terms. If you can create a solid and mutually rewarding foundation with your customer, the rest of the relationship will be smooth.

**Effective Communication.** Many customers will discontinue business with you simply because they are confused about something or misunderstand your contract. Effective communication is key to a healthy relationship. As a representative of your business, you should be involved in, and dedicated to, the satisfaction and growth of customer relationships within your business. When working with customers, know why the customer selected you in the first place. Keep sight of customer goals and pursue those goals relentlessly to satisfy your customer. Chances are your customers have a good reason for wanting to work with your business or purchase your product or service. Ask what that is and why, today of all days, they chose to make the move.

Most customers already believe they know what they want, very often they do not want your opinion, and want only for you to provide them with the product or service requested. While this is often ok, you should still try and understand what they are trying to achieve, or you may end up with poor reviews and an upset customer who feels they wasted their time. It all comes down to staying focused on the goals of the customer and the strategies for achieving those goals. Two primary questions to consider asking customers when attempting to understand their goals include:

- What is your goal for using or purchasing this product or service?
- What results are you expecting by using this product or service?

Asking these questions will help demonstrate a genuine concern for your customers and they will, most often, appreciate your sincerity.

## RELATIONSHIP MARKETING

Strong customer relationships are essential for your business if you desire to increase sales and generate a positive brand reputation. Customers frequently recognize their relationships with businesses similar to personal connections. In analyzing whether customers looking for relationships with businesses actually desired a genuine personal relationship with the business, it was found that a majority of business-to-customer (B2C) relationships were inauthentic when contrasted with genuine person-to-person relationships.[1]

The foundation of relationship marketing includes four essential elements of relationships that include commitment, trust, comprehension, and quality. In an examination of 306 online surveys, researchers confirmed that each of the four

[1] Bettencourt, L. A., Blocker, C. P., Houston, M. B., & Flint, D. J. (2015). Rethinking customer relationships. Business Horizons, 58, 99-108. doi:10.1016/j.bushor.2014.09.003

elements of relationships influenced customer loyalty. Nevertheless, the customer's perception and comprehension of quality and value influenced the relationship and purchase intentions. [2]

As a business, you need to identify your target customers by analyzing their lifestyles, psychographics, income, spending capabilities, and mentalities so that you may offer them relevant products and services. For example, knowing that individuals from lower income groups would never be interested in, or have the means to buy, expensive and luxurious products is beneficial in that it allows your business to focus its attention on the likely buyers of your product or service. Trying to sell a Mercedes or a luxury watch to someone who finds it difficult to make ends meet would definitely be a disastrous marketing technique.

## CUSTOMER BEHAVIOR

Customer behavior refers to the study of the purchasing tendencies of customers. Understanding the buying behaviors of customers will help you better market and sell your products or services to your targeted customers. It's important that you understand what prompts your customers to purchase a particular product as well as what keeps them from making a purchase. Understanding the behaviors of your customers will additionally assist in comprehending the decision-making stages your customers go through before making a purchase. Generally, there are several stages your customer goes through before they finally make a purchase. Other factors, be they cultural, social,

[2] Jussila, J. J., Kärkkäinen, H., & Aramo-Immonen, H. (2014). Social media utilization in business-to-business relationships of technology industry firms. Computers in Human Behavior, 30, 606-613. doi:10.1016/j.chb.2013.07.047

personal, or psychological, also influence the buying decision.

To help understand customer behaviors in an online environment, a study consisting of 350 customers concluded that customers' attitudes and behaviors toward businesses depended on their perceptions of the business, the product, ease of use, and convenience. [3] Establishing an understanding of the behaviors of your customers is central to developing successful marketing strategies. Analyzing customer behavior is vital for exploring opportunities that help in the development of successful strategies that influence customer decisions and expand brand awareness. Moreover, attempting to offer a product without understanding customer behavior could cause a loss of both revenue and time.

**Social Behaviors.** Understanding customers' social behaviors are valuable for gaining insights into human motivations and how customers allocate resources in various circumstances when making purchasing decisions. Your business could benefit from learning about the social behaviors of your customers as a means to direct marketing correspondence and impact customer behavioral attitudes.

**Personal Values.** In the context of business marketing, personal values are defined as an underlying determinant of the attitudes and behaviors of customers. In addition to social behaviors, personal values were found to have a significant influence on customer behaviors. However, personal values were noted to have a more significant effect on customer behavior compared to other psychographics considering personal values link centrally to an individual's cognitive system.

---

[3] Lim, W. M. (2013). Toward a theory of online buyer behavior using structural equation modeling. Modern Applied Science, 7, 34. doi:10.5539/mas.v7n10p34

# TYPES OF CUSTOMERS

Customers play a significant role in the success or failure of your business. In fact, the customer is the actual boss in all dealings and responsible for profits generated for your business. The customer is the one who uses the products and services and judges the quality of those products and services. Hence, it's important for your business to prioritize and retain former customers as well as continually gain new customers to sustain and grow the business. A strategy to gain new customers includes segmenting your current customers into groups which will help determine how to satisfy and attract your desired customer group.

Your segmenting strategy should also take into account:

- Age group of the customers
- Geographical location
- Lifestyle of customers
- Social status of customers

### Targeting the Right Customers

All customers fall within select groups, and it is your responsibility to know which group that is. It is also essential to know if you are reaching your desired targeted group(s). For example, funky designs and loud colors would be a hit among teenagers, whereas middle aged and the elderly would prefer subtle colors and sophisticated designs. Suits and khakis are extremely popular amongst men, whereas females prefer blazers and blouses. Know your target groups and plan accordingly.

### Customers are often of the following types:

**Loyal Customers**. These customers may be less in number but promote higher sales and profit as compared to other customers. These customers are generally satisfied with your product or service and desire consistency and reliability. Loyal customers often require individual attention and rewards that demand quality customer service.

**Discount Customers**. Discount customers are also frequent visitors but they usually only make purchases when offered discounts on regular products and brands or buy only low-cost products. The greater the discount, the more likely this customer is to purchase.

**Impulsive Customers**. These customers are difficult to market to as they don't have any specific item on their purchase list. Handling these customers is a challenge as they don't look for particular products and are attracted to businesses that have many options to choose from with products and prices on display.

**Wandering Customers**. These customers are likely to generate the least profit as they are not sure of what they want to purchase or *if* they want to purchase. Additionally, these customers don't usually have the finances available to make a purchase but may purchase at a later date dependent on whether they are still interested and have not found a better value elsewhere.

As you can see in the explanations above, loyal and repeat customers are ideal for most businesses. Nonetheless, it is necessary for you to study the behaviors of customers in your chosen demographic before connecting with them as it will help you to identify specific customer needs and respond accordingly. By identifying the behaviors of customers, you can easily create targeted strategies to attract and satisfy their wants and needs.

**Customer Profiling**: Customer profiling is a behavioral relationship marketing technique which involves a variety of marketing strategies ranging from simplistic to complex.

Customer profiling begins with the identification of data associated with satisfied existing customers and then uses that data as a basis to target new prospects with similar profiles. The profiles of customers can be categorized in multiple ways according to influential variables present in their profile.

Profiling consists of determining the characteristics and demographics of customers. Identifying demographic profiles of current customers may help your business strategize ways to attract new customers and generate higher revenue through targeted marketing strategies. To gather demographic information from existing customers, your business should track sales data and other customer related information to help determine the ideal customer for your business.

Customers have unique preferences and needs and segmenting allows for managing customers based on their individual or grouped characteristics. Invalid segmenting could produce dissatisfied customers. Customer profiling should be the basis of your segmenting strategy and has proved to be the most useful strategy in customer acquisition.

**Cultural Uniformity**. Although it is rarely discussed in smaller businesses, analyzing the cultural differences between your customers can help in developing targeted marketing strategies. Cultural differences naturally exist and can greatly influence your marketing. Cultural differences may include customer locations, beliefs and cultural norms, lifestyle, income, and many other psychographic and demographic parameters. Additionally, it is important to consider online customers and the environment and culture of your website visitors as they often have a wider reach than brick-and-mortar locations. No matter the location, you may have to acknowledge cultural differences if you decide to change the way you do business, or if you plan to expand online, or to another region.

The targeted customer for your business was likely determined by who your business would like to attract. You should target your marketing efforts toward those individuals and businesses who would most likely utilize your products or services. If you want all customers and ethnicities to purchase services from your company, you may need to analyze your marketing strategy and determine how to make it attractive for all groups and cultures. The best method to understanding your customers is to conduct marketing research, which is discussed later within this book.

## CUSTOMER PERCEPTION

Customer perception is a significant predictor of customer purchasing outcomes. The customer's perception of your purchasing processes can influence your business's reputation and sales. Customers with a positive perception of your business will likely react differently to reviews posted by previous customers compared to customers that do not have a positive perception.

**Value Perception.** As a business, you should seek to position positive product knowledge at the beginning of your customers' journey. While attempting to examine the relationship between customer uncertainty reduction and value perception, I found that customer uncertainty about a business influenced the overall value perception of the selected businesses. To reduce the concern of potential customer uncertainty, your business should publicly display reviews and testimonials to assist in improving the value perception of your business.

# CHAPTER 2

## Giving Them What They Want

## BUILDING VALUE AND RETENTION

There are plenty of products and services on the market from which your customers could choose to make their purchases. Customers that select your business to purchase goods or services do so because of their overall perceived value of your business. Consequently, your business must produce value that connects to, and positively influences, the customer's perception. If the customer has a positive perception of your business, they are more likely to make a purchase and promote your services or product, which can translate into future sales.

Like most businesses, I assume that the goal of your marketing strategy is to generate profit and brand awareness; which means it has to identify the right type of customer. From a marketing perspective, there is no better customer than a repeat customer. Considering the cost of maintaining repeat customers is less than gaining new customers, the additional revenue could be used for increasing your business's competitive advantage. Consequently, building customer satisfaction and loyalty are paramount for retaining customers and increasing revenue.

### Meeting and Exceeding Customer Expectations

Most 5-star hotels maintain customer databases detailing the room order choices of their guests. If a guest has asked for a particular beverage to be kept in the mini bar, the next time that guest makes a reservation at the hotel the staff ensures that the beverage is stocked in the room. Such small gestures go a long way in making customers feel important.

It is necessary to interact and communicate with customers on a regular basis if you wish to increase the satisfaction of your customers. In these interactions, it is required to determine the customer's needs and then act to satisfy those needs accordingly. Even if you offer identical products within a competing market, satisfaction provides high customer retention rates. It's no secret that retailers offer frequent shopper rewards to increase customer satisfaction. Retailers do this for a reason— because it's a no brainer if you want customers to come back. Many high-end retailers also provide membership cards and discount benefits so that the customer remains loyal to their business.

## STAYING COMPETITIVE

Businesses lose customers for various reasons. I once lost a long-time customer of over 8 years, finding out only after realizing I was locked out of their hosting account. These things happen, and they happen for several reasons, but mostly, customers discontinue business because they feel they aren't satisfied with current results.

A competitor swooping in at a local event and making new promises becomes an easily tempting proposition for your customer who hasn't heard from you in a while. Just think, if you aren't providing for your customer someone else will. Just as in personal dating relationships, if you don't show interest and pay attention, there is always someone else waiting to take your place.

Customers can also easily be attracted to another business who simply excites them because that business presents something new and different. Nearly every year, businesses and customers will want to change how they do business. They will have new resolutions, new plans, and new strategies for success, and they will want to partner with a company or individual just as excited to fulfill their goals and take their business to the next level. During this time, you can't simply offer the same products or services that you have always offered.

Generally, throughout the year, or at least once a year, you should make certain that you introduce or update your customers on new services and offerings. At the end of the year, your customers will be speaking with family and friends during the holidays. Those family and friends will offer business references, discuss new trends, or may even offer to do the work themselves for a lower price. Customers will also be attending local business events and parties, and everyone at these events will have a million ways of convincing your customer that there is a better and cheaper solution for them.

**Brand Evangelists.** A happy customer is likely to tell their friends and family of the service they received. Creating brand evangelists doesn't necessarily involve rewarding the customer with free products or services. The best method for building loyalty and creating brand evangelists is by letting the customer know that they are appreciated as a customer and that you enjoy referrals.

Satisfied customers are also likely to spread the word through social media about the service they received from your company without being asked. If they are happy, they will likely tell everyone why they are. Customer satisfaction goes a long way when creating brand evangelists. You can identify a brand evangelist by joining and staying current with social networks and watching for your business name to be mentioned on those networks. Another great opportunity for building evangelists is to get involved with customers online by incorporating widgets into your company website. These widgets can be used to allow for site visitors to communicate their thoughts and share them on their favorite social networking websites with the click of a button.

### Customer Loyalty and Satisfaction

Most businesses believe that a satisfied customer is also a loyal customer. That is not always the case, as your customer can be satisfied and not loyal to your business. Satisfaction is an emotion while loyalty is related to a future action taken by the customer.

Building satisfied and loyal customers require:

- Keeping customers engaged in the sales process
- Educating customers on why they should choose you over your competition
- Knowing the unique needs of your customers and satisfying those needs

Not every customer is destined to be a life-long customer— but if you follow the tactics above, both you and your customer will be set up for a happy and productive relationship.

### Understanding your customer loyalty level.

**Satisfied but disloyal customers**: A customer can be

fully satisfied but may not be loyal due to following reasons:

**Experimental Customer.** These types of customers like to experiment and enjoy the option of diverging in other available businesses in the market.

**Price Shopper.** These customers are happy with your product or service but will only use your service until they are comfortable in duplicating your results at a lower price.

**Business Growth.** These customers may feel that your methods or product and services are outdated, and will go to a different business that markets having and using the latest trends and technology to grow with the customer's goals.

**Unsatisfied but loyal customers**: The other situation is when the customer is loyal but is unsatisfied. The reasons for this are:

**Lack of available options**: This situation can arise if your business does not offer products or services offered by competitors or when your business offers an inferior service.

**Emotionally connected**: There are some customers who are afraid to change their supplier because of an emotional business attachment or bonding. The customer may feel that it would be best to try and fix an unsatisfied situation rather than start new.

For your business to be successful, it is important for you to gain customer loyalty. While satisfaction may not guarantee loyalty, it *is* a prerequisite.

### Customer Satisfaction

According to a study of 362 marketing agencies, 95% of the agencies believed they placed a priority on the needs of their customers. Additionally, 80% believed they delivered a superior customer experience. While businesses may believe they place a priority on customer services, the same study found that only 8% of customers agreed that these businesses prioritized customer service.[4]

The relationship between businesses and customers are often one-sided. Where businesses may only see customers as numbers, customers want to be seen as individuals. Creating genuine customer experiences are about providing a unique value, surpassing expectations, engaging customers, and remaining honest.

Successful businesses find ways to satisfy and build customer relationships, as they should. Customers are spending their money to partner and invest with your business. They are your brand ambassadors who will promote your business to their friends and family. You should make it a priority to satisfy their needs and concerns. You can help your business get ahead if you can master the art of customer relationships and build loyal followers.

## QUALITY RELATIONSHIPS

A periodic marketing and customer audit are required if you want to enhance the quality of services and products that your

---

[4] "Tuning In to the Voice of Your Customer," Harvard Management Update, Vol. 10, No. 10, October 2005.

business offers to its customers. Delivering top quality services to customers is considered the most effective way to ensure that your business stands out from its competitors. The main ingredients that are involved in a quality relationship between your customer and your business are **trust** and **commitment**.

**Trust.** Trust refers to confidence and security in relationships and should be treated as the biggest investment in building long term relationships. As a result of understanding and addressing your customers' needs, any doubts of whether or not your business respects them, and is sincere, are relieved and demonstrates that you are a reliable partner. A lack of trust, on the other hand, weakens the relationship, and as a result, the likelihood of uncertainty and disloyalty increases.

**Commitment.** Commitment is yet another milestone that should be achieved to create a long-term relationship. Commitment can only be attained when there is trust and the two parties share similar values. In a committed relationship, both your business and the customer wants the relationship to last considering the time and energy needed to switch to another business or market toward new customers.

Other attributes that promote a high-quality relationship include the following:

**Courtesy**. Many times, your customers may not be satisfied with your business or with the product or service that you offer. It is essential that you provide your customers with quality customer service during these times. Delivering positive and courteous responses act as a catalyst in driving customer satisfaction.

**Availability.** Most customers prefer human responses compared to automated emails or messages. Hence, it is important for your business to be available to customers with queries and needs. Being available also promotes emotional bonding between customers and your business which is beneficial for establishing and building a profitable business.

**Responsiveness**. Your business should always have prompt, responsive, and experienced employees serving your customers. If a potential customer calls and asks about some critical product feature and your employee fails to properly explain it or is non-responsive, the customer would likely contact a different business who will provide them with the answers to their questions.

**Current**. Always remain current with, and ahead of, your industry and changes in your market. Strategies, services, and products often advance or deteriorate with time due to competition and the higher cost of innovation. Consequently, your business should remain current and relevant to your customers and potential customers.

## EDUCATING = SATISFYING

Not all customers will understand the details of your product or the necessities of your service offering. It's important that you help educate your customers on your product and changes in the market relevant to your business. While you may not want to move away from your original contract, your competitors will try and attract your customers by introducing new tools, methods, and trends. To prevent your customers from moving to a competitor, you should setup and attend regular weekly or monthly meetings with your customers and go over what it is that you are doing for them and why. When asking your customers what they think about the quality of your product or service, don't be surprised if they ask about new technologies or trends and why you aren't using those methods. If you aren't aware of new changes or innovations, you should inform the customer that you will look into the technologies and present your findings to them.

## ATTRACTING THE RIGHT CUSTOMER

Many businesses that I have consulted for boasted about their low prices but hated the fact that customers would only purchase products on discount. Those businesses failed to sell products at a profitable margin and often could not afford other expenses including employees, marketing, and general operating costs. It's great when your customers love your low prices, but if your customers are the only ones winning, then that is not good for your business.

Most customers – the ones you want – will view your product or service as an investment. They likely will not see your prices as an issue considering they desire other conveniences of your business, which may include your location, quality, reputation, etc. That's a very different mindset from that of customers who simply want to buy a product at the lowest cost possible. However, it is your responsibility to market your overall *value* as the focus of your business and not just your prices.

**Qualifying The Customer.** I've seen it often; an employee talks with a potential customer and the customer seems (or acts) interested. After that meeting, the employee is confident about what the customer wants and offers the customer pretty much everything that the company sells, backtracking from pricing individual services to a grand total number.

The problem? The potential customer has never purchased from the business and has no plans to make a purchase until the end of the year. In addition, his budget is way below what the employee proposed. Immediately, the customer disregards the business as an option, both now and when his budget increases by 50% the following year.

Sometimes, a customer will never be the right fit. And sometimes it just isn't the right time. Don't ruin your chances by not understanding your customers' current and *future* needs – including their financial constraints. In addition to understanding your customers' objectives and the current state of your marketing outreach, you should also define the following:

- What are the customer's goals?
- What does success for the overall company look like?
- What is the timeframe for achieving those goals?
- Are there separate long-term and short-term goals?
- What specific metrics will define success?
- What challenge is the customer currently facing?
- What value does the customer see in the services you provide?

**Emotional Connection.** Customers want to do business with businesses they like. It's that simple. While we shouldn't have to emphasize this fact, we sometimes forget that emotions often drive our purchasing decisions, not logic. When sending marketing material to customers, you have to first develop rapport with those customers, or else your marketing will simply become another "to review" item on customers' lists. Start with a call or a coffee meeting. Find commonalities. Listen to the customer's challenges. Show them appreciation and gain their trust. Then, send the marketing material with a personal note and a reminder of some shared moment.

**Be a Partner.** The customer doesn't always know best – even if they think they do. If you truly want to be a partner (not simply an order taker), you need to understand if what the customer wants will get them the results they need. These are obviously two very different things. As a partner, you need to challenge the customer by letting them know when there are better products or more efficient and effective ways to be productive. This is also how your business can stand out in competitive situations.

In marketing, if the potential customer wants SEO and social media services, and you simply send marketing outlining why you are the best agency for providing SEO and social media, your marketing material will be similar to every other business's marketing – except for that one agency that considers why the customer believes they need SEO and social media and what actually makes sense for the customer's goal, budget, and timeline. You can stand out by taking this different approach through questioning your customers' actual needs and goals which would allow you to offer them the optimal product or service solution for their needs.

**Framing Your Price**. You need confidence to make a sale – and you need that same confidence in the product or service that you are selling. Most business strategies are designed so that customers are given the bare-bones option first, and then the business reveals what it can do for its Super Special, Super-Charged Retainer or its "Everything you ever dreamed of" package. By giving your lowest price first and then the higher price, you are cautiously approaching the customer with the idea that they should spend more for a complete service, but not convincing them which package is right for them or their business.

Consider this: which of the following statements is most impactful? You'll save $1,000 if you buy marketing automation software. Or; You'll lose 100 customers if you don't buy marketing automation software. People feel much stronger about the thought of losing something. When you set up your business strategy, emphasize the possible loses if the customer does not take action now. In addition, set up your marketing so that the right package is presented first. Then, if necessary, outline what a stripped-down version of this would cost. Also, emphasize how much more difficult, time consuming, or unattainable achieving the customer's goals will be if they choose the cheaper version. You're not really changing anything about what you do. You're just reframing the conversation.

**Outline The Process**. Every customer's goals and challenges are unique, but that doesn't mean you need to start from scratch when building a sales strategy. If you have a keen understanding of what you do, how to sell it, and how to package it, you should be able to create or customize an existing sales strategy to fit the needs of, and attract, any type of customer. However, this relies on your business having a repeatable and defined selling process. When questioning your customers, you should know:

- The goals, plans, and challenges of the customer
- Current customer metrics and key company information
- The cost to the customer of not doing anything to meet their goals

When building a sales strategy to target your desired customer, the strategy should include:

- o Campaign goals
- o Scope of services and benefits
- o Reporting
- o Success Metrics
- o Timeline
- o Budget

With this framework in place and a defined process for gathering information, it will be much easier to put together a winning sales and marketing strategy.

**Set Expectations**. Once you have confirmed that the customer is a good fit for your business and the customer has requested more information and an estimate, you need to detail what the purchasing or contract phase looks like. The price estimate or sales collateral is the next step in the commitment process on the part of the customer. It should confirm everything you have already spoken about and solidify the deal.

There is no magic trick to selling. There shouldn't be some big reveal. There is no tool for convincing and impressing. The price estimate or contract proposal is a confirmation, in writing, of what your business can do, how it will do it, when it will be completed, and why the customer specifically needs your product or services. It should be the final step prior to a contract being signed, and your business and the customer should both be confident that the deal will close – and soon.

**The Follow-Up**. Providing the customer with a price isn't the final step – obviously. You still need the potential customer to make the purchase. Because many businesses don't like to think outside of an immediate sale, they often fail to implement follow-up procedures that pay off after an estimate. They give up after a few emails or calls. Remember: Persistence is key. If you understand your customers' journey, you know that this is all a part of the decision-making process. Now, you just need to give potential customers the information they need to make the final leap.

To help with your follow-up, create a process for your typical sales cycle armed with information on average close rates and the time it takes to complete a deal. With a customer relationship management program (CRM), you can define these stages and easily keep track of progress. Map out what information you will send at each part in the process. Consider creating an email series that checks in on the customer every few weeks and reiterates how your business can help. Send the proposal with an invitation for an in-person meeting, visit, or phone call the following week to continue the momentum of the conversations. Tweak the messaging of your emails to determine what resonates with prospects. You've gotten this far. Don't fail at the follow-up.

**Building Trust**. Trust takes time. When you are sending marketing material to a potential customer, there just isn't always time to create a trusting relationship. But there are things you can do to prove you are credible, which is a step in the right direction. Credibility starts with a good reputation and a good design which inspires confidence in the viewer. When designing, follow modern design standards and practices to create a clean, easy-to-read campaign. In addition, marketing content full of misspellings and poor grammar can be a red flag for customers. It says little for your business's ability to pay attention to detail and reduces your credibility as a professional organization. Finally, you need compelling testimonials or case studies that showcase the results you can deliver, the type of working relationships you have, and how you solved problems for previous customers.

CHAPTER **3**

## Always Look Your Best

# BRAND STRATEGY

## BRANDING BENEFITS

To say that you need a brand to be successful is inaccurate. The laundry mat or embroidery shop up the street do not have a brand and they are doing very well. Whether you need a brand is dependent on the goal of your business. For example, if you are a service based business, or simply have a business that is in demand, then having a strong brand is not needed considering customers will seek you out and already know what they want, how they want it, and at what speed and price they want it. Think, where does the local school purchase its school buses? Have you ever seen a school bus manufacturer advertise their brand on television or at local events?

You do, however, need to have a brand if you have significant competition and if you have a niche product which requires educating customers. The goal of a brand is to provide customers with reasons to purchase your product or service over the competition. Without a solid brand, it makes marketing and customer acquisition expensive and time consuming. A brand gives your business its unique character – its look and feel, voice, and identity. Without its image, Nike is just one more shoemaker, and Macy's is simply another retailer. A good brand should have a foundation based on value and customer engagement. The brand should represent the mission of your business and hold relevancy to your customers.

**Perceived Value.** Your brand should reflect the goal of your business by highlighting your strengths and encouraging a positive perception. Perceived value influences the amount of money your customer believes your product or service is worth. Whether marketing a service or a product, the results are similar in that both rely on the customer's perception of your business's expertise, quality, and reputation.

If your business and your competitors sell the exact same item, built the same way, and from the same materials, it is likely that the business with the better brand value reputation will sell the item at a higher rate because of the perceived value by the customer. If your customer perceives the value of your brand as high, they will likely make assumptions that the products you promote are of high-quality as well.

## BRAND DEVELOPMENT

Your brand is often your business's most valuable asset. A strong brand can generate loyal customers and positive sales. The brand should be seen by customers as both positive and valuable. For your brand to be valuable to customers, it needs to simplify the decision-making process and reduce any perceived risk for your customers.

**Social Media Branding.** The personalized brand for your business should include a presentation of your unique benefits, knowledge, experience, and expertise that help make your business memorable. These unique assets influence customers to make a purchase and professionals to want to work with your brand. To expand brand awareness, start by creating, or cleaning up, your online presence and social media pages. On your social media pages, you should not post or subscribe to anything that does not enhance your brand. This includes both text and images. In addition to social media pages, you should create digital image galleries and a website showcasing the best of your brand.

## BRAND IMAGE

Find a good graphic artist. The right artist should not only be creative, but should also understand how to create artwork that is marketable. A well-designed business logo helps your customers remember your business, as customers tend to remember images better than they remember words. Designing your image is the easy part, but knowing what to design, who to design for, and how to direct, entertain, persuade, and attract attention with your artwork is the difference between having pretty artwork and effective artwork.

A logo can often look simple, but even the simplest logo may have taken weeks or months to create. Your logo deserves deep thought and continued editing until it is well-developed and ready to display as a unique image that enhances your brand and helps you stand out from the crowd.

When developing your logo, consider:

**Everybody Loves Custom Type.** While we're on the subject of being unique, there's almost nothing that can give your logo a unique feel quite like custom lettering. Too often, I see logo designs as simply a trip to the font menu to see which typeface makes the company name look best. Custom type helps ensure that your unique logo will stay that way. Dishonest designers will rip off your work in a heartbeat if they discover which typeface you're using, but it takes some real skill to mimic custom, hand-drawn type.

**Keep It Simple Stupid.** Let's face it, not everyone can bust out beautiful, hand-drawn script on a whim. Just because you're a designer doesn't mean you're an awesome illustrator or typographer (though it helps). If you fit this description, fear not, there's nothing preventing you from making awesome logos. In this situation, remember these four powerful words: Keep it simple stupid (K.I.S.S.)! Simple, but powerful logos permeate the business world and always prove to be the best icons.

**Know What It Means.** Every good logo has a story. Far beyond a pretty sketch, strong logos are filled with meaning, both obvious and hidden. It's great when you can talk about your business logo and have a quality and thoughtful story behind the brand image. When building your logo, make certain that it not only looks cool and attractive but that it also ties into the company's core values and mission. Furthermore, make sure that your logo can stand the test of time. No one wants a logo that will be outdated after a few years.

## DESIGN COLORS

One of the most important tools to take into consideration when designing your brand image is the color palette. This is not a superficial decision— color carries meaning and communicates ideas. Sometimes you're locked-in to the colors of a brand, but other times you'll have the freedom to explore.

Your visual identity is a visualization of your brand's

characteristics and includes your logo, color palette, typography, and more. Logo strategies are evolving in line with the rise in digital channels, available formats, and color options. Your logo should help your business stand out. According to Nielsen Research, when purchasing a product, more than 92% of customers place brand presentation as a determining factor in making a purchase.[5] Color is visual, it affects mood and humor, and triggers cognitive and emotional meaning for customers. The colors you select for your business should help to enhance your brand and influence, not hinder, sales.

When deciding upon a color palette to select for your brand, treat your colors no differently than you would your keywords. A balanced recipe equals impact. In other words, colors subconsciously effect customer perception and help to convince customers that they like what they see.

**Color Meanings and Significance:**

**Red**. Associated with energy, war, danger, strength, power, determination as well as passion, desire, and love. Red is a very emotionally intense color. It enhances human metabolism, increases respiration rate, and raises blood pressure.

**Pink**. Signifies romance, love, and friendship. It denotes feminine qualities and passiveness.

**Brown**. Suggests stability and denotes masculine qualities.

**Orange**. Represents enthusiasm, fascination, happiness, creativity, determination, attraction, success, encouragement, and stimulation. Orange has very high visibility, so you can

---

[5] http://www.nielsen.com/us/en/insights/news/2012/consumer-trust-in-online-social-and-mobile-advertising-grows.html

use it to catch attention and highlight the most important elements of your design. Orange is very effective for promoting food products and toys.

**Gold**. Evokes the feeling of prestige. The meaning of gold is illumination, wisdom, and wealth. Gold often symbolizes high quality.

**Yellow**. Associated with joy, happiness, intellect, and energy. Produces a warming effect, arouses cheerfulness, stimulates mental activity, and generates muscle energy.

**Green**. The color of nature. It symbolizes growth, harmony, freshness, and fertility. Green has strong emotional correspondence with safety. Green has great healing power. It is the most restful color for the human eye; it can improve vision.

**Blue**. Associated with depth and stability. It symbolizes trust, loyalty, wisdom, confidence, intelligence, and truth. Blue is considered beneficial to the mind and body. Blue is strongly associated with tranquility and calmness.

**Purple**. Purple combines the stability of blue and the energy of red. Purple is associated with royalty. It symbolizes power, nobility, luxury, and ambition. It conveys wealth and extravagance. Purple is associated with wisdom, dignity, independence, creativity, mystery, and magic.

**White**. White is associated with light, goodness, innocence, purity, and virginity. It is considered to be the color of perfection. White means safety, purity, and cleanliness. In advertising, white is associated with coolness and cleanliness.

**Black**. Black is associated with power, elegance, formality, death, evil, and mystery. It is considered to be a very formal, elegant, and prestigious color.

## BRAND STORY

As humans, one of the ways we build relationships is through the stories we tell; why else do we catch up with our friends, right? In business, it's no different. You want to create moments between your business and your customers. Those willing to share the experiences of their founders, customers, and staff can reap the many benefits that storytelling offers. It shifts the focus a little from what you do and talks about why you do it. The story of your brand is as individual as you are, and it needs to tell your audience who you are and why you're doing what you do. It is where your manifesto comes to life, giving your audience context for your business and a chance to connect with what is important to you. After all, people buy from people.

## PERSONAL BRAND MESSAGING

Branding involves creating, maintaining, and enhancing the awareness of your product or service. In establishing the credibility and awareness of your brand, third-party endorsements have a tremendous effect. Individual branding is different from business branding in that it requires a continued positive attitude and even stronger relationship building. Unlike business branding, which recommends posting a social ad or banner on a webpage, billboard, or in print collateral, personal branding requires networking— and lots of it. Networking can be done via social networks, local group meetings, and events. In addition, during these networking sessions, the individual needs to be likable and must present good character, knowledge, and a pleasant appearance.

Attitudes toward the message of your brand have an impact on the customer's purchase and behavioral intentions. To promote your brand, you could invest in advertising, which is a more general means of communication for promoting your brand. Marketing-oriented publicity elicits either positive or negative cognitive responses in customers. A positive cognitive response enhances the brand messaging which has an impact on the customer's purchasing decision. A negative attitude and cognitive response toward brand messaging reduce the likelihood of a customer making a purchase.

A perfect example of marketing based on customer brand attitude and the use of endorsements is the Beats headphone brand. The brand was introduced without a large budget and focused on building credibility through celebrity endorsements and word-of-mouth. As customers accepted the credibility as positive, they spread the word about the product as being a commodity to those interested in owning the popular brand. With the help of social promotions, celebrity credibility, industry targeted publicity, and brand messaging the brand has developed into a multi-billion dollar company.

## PRIVATE/WHITE LABELING

If providing your product to private label retailers, you may be concerned about competition and losing revenue. However, if you choose not to provide your product to private label retailers, another brand likely will. An online study consisting of 1,600 customers found that brand imitation by private labels increased a customers' preference relative to the imitated brand. However, the study also found that if the private label retailer used its name on the imitated national brand, it did not hurt the sales or reputation of the national brand, but may have negatively affected the private labels' brand image and reputation.[6]

Private label products account for more than 30% of global

[6] Aribarg, A., Arora, N., Henderson, T., & Youngju, K. (2014). Private Label Imitation of a National Brand: Implications for Consumer Choice and Law. Journal Of Marketing Research, 51(6), 657-675. doi:10.1509/jmr.13.0420

grocery sales. Although there are individuals who are cautious about their purchasing decisions, there are also many shoppers who shop based on name recognition and perceived value. Within the United Kingdom, for example, private label production rose from 21.5% in 1980 to 39.3% in 2003.[7] The success of private labels throughout the world has presented challenges to international brands concerning budgets, advertising, and sales.

An example of national and private label products are over-the-counter medicines. While a national brand may present a televised commercial or a print advertisement, the private brand offers little or no promotional efforts. In this regard, the national brand should sell fairly well based on their marketing efforts. Regarding the private brand, individuals who purchase private brands likely do so because they are not affected by marketing efforts and are attracted to the lower cost. Consequently, if your business can earn revenue by providing to private labels, you will not necessarily lose a customer or profits. Whether you lose revenue is determined by the real value of the product. Regarding working with private labels, your business would be responsible for product sourcing, advertising, warehousing, and promotional efforts. If you can generate higher profits from selling the same product under a different name, and still have your current business, what's the harm?

The main difference between private label and national brand awareness is the brand's marketing and advertising efforts. Marketing generates familiarity to customers, and the assumption is that the perceptual response patterns are different toward private labels than national brands. One important factor is that private labels lack outside advertising which affects product knowledge and sales. Customers are likely to purchase a national

---

[7] Lamey, L., Deleersnyder, B., Dekimpe, M. G., & Steenkamp, J. E. (2007). How Business Cycles Contribute to Private-Label Success: Evidence from the United States and Europe. Journal Of Marketing, 71(1), 1-15. doi:10.1509/jmkg.71.1.1

brand if they believe the private labels are of lower quality. National brands often sell more product than private labels considering customers perceive that national brands have a better quality than private labels. Wonder bread, for instance, may not use the same quality materials for private labels as it does for its national brand. Additionally, the company may use a different formula or materials that are not as fresh.

Large national brands seek customers with a higher level of knowledge than private labels. By promoting their brand, national brands enjoy customers that are loyal and who are likely to promote their products. In addition, national brand customers often purchase based on cues from their memory of the brand. For instance, if a customer were to arrive at a retail shelf to purchase a box of cereal, they are likely to purchase the box that reminds them of something they have seen or with which they have a positive perception. In this instance, the national brand is the likely choice of the customer considering the national brand generally has a larger marketing budget and will be more familiar to the shopper.

## CHAPTER **4**

# You Built It; They Still Ain't Coming

## WEBSITE INFLUENCE

### WEBSITE

A website gives your business the opportunity for exposure 24-hours a day, 7 days a week. There is no other medium that allows consumers to discover all of the benefits of your business, at their convenience, and provide a source for direct correspondence from the user to you in real time. The benefits of a website are limitless.

**Building Process.** When building a website, make certain that you design the site for your customer and not for you or the graphic artist or designer. Design for the individuals that will use the site. By building for your customers, it allows you to target who is actually going to be viewing, and hopefully purchasing, from the website. Don't design for looks, but for a purpose. If customers don't like the colors then, no matter what you or your designer may think, those colors need to be changed. When building a website, you need to focus on attracting your target audience and making the site user-friendly.

A properly built website requires an effective title and meta tags, incoming links, and a strong architectural design. In addition, you should implement social media strategies through the use of proper link baiting, keywords, and creating a pay-per click campaign that will increase customer conversions.

A strategy that I have found to work well in improving website conversions includes adding an online blog or newsgroup. This method has shown to be a positive step in influencing conversions as well as conversations. In addition, it helps to generate a higher domain authority when utilizing unique content which can benefit the site's ranking within search engines. Furthermore, blogs and news updates elevate customer satisfaction and attract traffic to your website.

Another question that should be asked when building your website is, "Does my website compete with my competitors?" and "Does it target my desired customer group?" If you don't have your website built by a designer who understands your industry, then the answers are likely to be, "No." Your website needs to represent you and your business. If it looks cheap, so will your business. If you try to cut corners, your customers will know. It's better to have no website at all than a badly designed, poorly built website that doesn't represent your business in a positive light, doesn't serve the needs of your customers, and doesn't drive traffic.

## CONTENT MANAGEMENT SYSTEMS

Having fresh content is mandatory if your intent is to drive traffic to your site to gain new and repeat customers. With a CMS, you can keep your website updated with the latest news, articles, products, and services. A CMS provides you with full control to manage the content on your website.

**Updating**. A CMS allows your website to have new content added on a regular basis and be easily upgraded with the latest technology as it becomes available. Additionally, a CMS gives you full control so that you can easily add new updates and blogs to your website without having to call a programmer to do it for you.

With a CMS, you can easily implement, update, and manage:

- Article publishing
- Website forums
- Photo galleries
- Surveys and polls
- Interactive event calendars
- Complex data entry forms

**Management**. Through the use of a CRM, website content can be managed through a simple user interface that allows for quick task completion. The administration area of a CRM is often easy to use and can involve multiple access levels for various employees and management control.

## E-COMMERCE

E-commerce and online transactions account for billions of dollars in sales activity. While e-commerce is a good opportunity for your business to expand online, it could be overwhelming if your business is not prepared for online growth. Initiating your online store is like opening a second location, so you will need to hire new employees and a new technology team to help manage the new location. Additionally, your online store will require top-notch security measures, privacy resolutions, and excellent customer support. You will need to define and understand your new online customer group which will be very different from those ordering by phone or shopping in-store. If your customers are within an older demographic group, you could find yourself having to create and market your new business service to a new user group from scratch considering disruptive technology is often influenced and adopted by younger demographics.

The benefits of e-commerce are based on the efficiency of the automated system. Benefits include a decrease in overall production and transaction costs if implemented properly which can help resolve business concerns regarding the budget. Ample stock inventories, proper notifications, timely delivery dates, and excellent customer support is key to achieving e-commerce success.

A drawback of e-commerce versus brick-and-mortar businesses is that with e-commerce sites it is difficult to generate a sale through user interaction with the business. To partially resolve this issue, you can implement a chat system and monitor the effects of your e-commerce strategies by using activity and traffic tools that monitor users visiting the website.

## MOBILE OPTIMIZATION

Some businesses have websites but don't have a properly built website that is optimized for mobile devices. Even if you do have a mobile website, customers may complain that the website doesn't look as good or that the website's performance on mobile devices is sluggish. When you're building your mobile website keep in mind that it's on a phone, or device smaller than a computer monitor, meaning your buttons need to be bigger, some content needs to be moved, and some content needs to be removed or blocked from being seen on the mobile version of the website. A mobile website should be a watered-down version of your main website and should include only key selling points and a call to action. Keep in mind that most mobile users aren't on your website to view your special graphics or large photo gallery. If your site is not built or optimized specifically for mobile users, your bounce rate will skyrocket and you'll lose a potential customer over a fixable problem.

# WEBSITE TRAFFIC

There are two ways to gain customers for your website or business. The first way is to pay for it. You could easily pay a marketer, advertiser, or branding company and gain customers that way. The other way is to earn your customers. This is the way that I believe works best and the one that I practice. To earn customers, you must get to know them. You should know where they go, which websites they visit, and local events they attend. This doesn't just consist of putting your name and business card in these locations, but it involves you interacting with them and finding a true understanding of their lifestyle and preferences, and what it is that they desire from a business such as yours.

**Alien Traffic.** A study by Incapsula, one of the leading web security services and optimizers, unearthed that more than half of your website traffic could be alien. Not exactly the ones portrayed in War of the Worlds, but maybe. The findings released suggested that around 31% of website traffic was harmful and includes spammers, spies, scrappers, and hackers.[8]

Then there are the 20% of friendly visitors such as Google Bot as well as other search engine indexers. What this means is that analytics do not provide the whole picture and human

[8] http://www.bizepic.com/2014/12/19/shocking-half-website-traffic-2014-bot-traffic/

visitors are not alone prowling the internet. To mitigate this, you should make security a part of your online marketing undertaking and tighten your website content with relevant keywords for the friendly indexers so your website is pulled by more human traffic based on the intent of website visitors.

## SEARCH ENGINE OPTIMIZATION

SEO is about optimizing your website to increase traffic by improving internal and external strategies that will ultimately increase site traffic to your website. Businesses that practice SEO can vary, and there are many unique elements to consider when optimizing a website. The goal of SEO is to discover the search terms and phrases needed to build and generate website traffic. Don't worry, if you're confused about this, you are not alone.

Most web traffic is guided by three major search engines (Google, Bing, and Yahoo!). If your site isn't found by search engines or your content isn't optimized enough to be picked-up by their databases, you lose a great opportunity of marketing your website to potential clients or customers. Whether your site provides services, content, information, or products search engines are a primary navigation method for almost all internet users. Experience and statistics have proven that search engine traffic can make (or break) a website's or business' success. SEO targeted website visitors provide revenue, publicity, and exposure like no other. Investing in SEO, whether through finances or time, can create an exceptional rate of return.

**Working With SEO.** To create a successful website with proper SEO, you must first be sure that the website is well built as it plays a significant role in how search engines analyze your domain rank and relevancy. In creating your website, you must first be sure that the website is appealing to the customer and that the site is easily navigable. The way to create the proper architecture for a website is to build a site that is flat and has minimum clicks necessary for the user to get to the destination page.

In addition to creating the proper navigational structure of the website, you must also check for broken internal and external links. There are many useful tools for finding broken links which will crawl through your website and recognize any broken links that forward to 404 or corrupted pages. Another technique for improving the architecture of your website is to check the server header response code and duplicate content. If either of these is found, they should be corrected. While some of the concerns may need to be fixed by the sites developer, others can be fixed by simply changing some wording or taking the proper steps with search engines to correct the information.

Finally, make sure that your website has the proper architecture and has one main URL by setting up a canonical 301 redirect if needed to change www... to non-www. To search engines, having your site accessible by both looks like two different websites and your domain authority may be negatively affected. In addition, be sure to remove any developmental site that was used to originally create the website. By leaving the developmental website on its server, this creates duplicate content that can get crawled by search engines and create a negative impact on your main website. Once the live site is up and running, the developmental site should be taken down and removed from search engines if it exists.

An SEO campaign is based on the cornerstone of on-page optimization. However, when it comes to which on-page SEO techniques really work, there are 8 opinions for every 5 experts. When your business is at stake, you can't just optimize your website and hope that it works. You need to be completely confident that everything you do will help your rankings. Moreover, you need to be sure that you've done everything on the SEO checklist and your website is optimized across the board.

# BACKLINKING

To help build the authority and rank of your website, you should establish quality backlinks on niche websites, and not just broad or directory websites. By including links on sites relevant to your own, you will positively help your website ranking and attract new customers. In addition to niche websites, your backlinks should include sites with a high page rank. Link building strategies can easily come from participating in blogs, online forums, and local event groups. When placing a backlink on these sites, you should utilize unique keywords and descriptive anchor text. Another option to find credible backlinks is to search your competitors' link groupings. A link grouping is a page on the internet from which all, or most, of your competitors get incoming links. By searching your targeted keywords, common backlinks of your competitors can be located. Once these backlinks are identified, you should visit and include your website link on these websites if possible. If these websites are a relevant niche to your business, it should produce favorable results.

# WEBSITE MARKETING

While social media sites are great for blogging and news updates, you should also include the blog text and updates on your business website so that it creates more content and attracts attention from search engines. By utilizing blogs and newsgroups to attract website visitors, you can create an effective strategy which will help gain and increase website click-through rates and the length of time users spend on your website. This could ultimately help with increasing search engine credibility and domain authority. In addition, including keywords and descriptions in image ALT tags on your website will create an extremely effective strategy that is not only beneficial for improving content search results but will also boost your rank in image search directories.

You should additionally include an easy bookmark feature on your website. By including a bookmark widget, you can gain customer loyalty and rank better with search engines that index bookmark websites such as Del.icio.us and Google bookmarks.

To create a strategy that will encourage customer interactivity, you can also setup email marketing and newsletter campaigns along with creating polls and surveys to gain customer feedback and help enhance the experience of your customers. Newsletters could include information on upcoming specials, events, and changes in the business that could benefit the customer.

Links for allowing customers to opt out of receiving emails and referring a friend for discounts should also be included in each newsletter. Your business can benefit by tracking the results of email campaigns using newsletter and website tracking tools such as Google Analytics. By viewing monthly reports, you will be able to see which keywords, content, and paid campaigns are most effective. In addition, it will allow for you to see where visitors come from, how long they visit a certain web page, the last page they viewed before leaving your website, and how your stats compare to the industry benchmarks.

## THE INTERNET

With the internet changing and advancing to web 2.0 technologies, your business has the opportunity to be marketed on broad online networks including social media platforms such as Facebook, Twitter, Instagram, and LinkedIn. To create success within the web 2.0 market, you need to join online social environments and create brand awareness in a positive way. With thousands of social networking sites, blogs, and forums across the internet, you have a great opportunity to build your brand. With the development of new website techniques and the growth of online networking, the internet has become the largest marketing tool to build and grow businesses. You can create success with the internet through a combination of online marketing, customer referrals, and through satisfied customers promoting your brand online through social media.

**Internet marketing** gives your business the advantage of appealing to customers in a medium that has the power to deliver results instantly. Internet marketing is the key to having your website found by customers. Without marketing, your website may randomly be found once everyone couple of days or months, but it will not generate high revenue. You need to create as much exposure as possible to gain more customers. Just like a great job resume, it's no good if you don't send it out to employers. The same goes for creating a great website and not marketing it. If you can't be found, you will not gain new customers. Internet marketing is relatively inexpensive, and your business can reach a wide audience at a fraction of the cost of traditional advertising budgets.

## BLOGGING STRATEGY

A blog or weblog covers a mixture of what is happening in the daily life of your business as well as new and upcoming events. A blogging strategy can be used to help determine how to engage with online users and generate website traffic. When designing your blog, be sure to create it so that it increases brand awareness and attracts readers.

Other benefits of blogging include:

- Google loves it! Blogs are great for increasing website indexed pages, and Google places value on websites with a high volume of indexed pages.

- Customers can remain current with the status of your business events and updates. Additionally, a blog can define your brand as authoritative and help your business be seen as professional and knowledgeable.

## ARTICLES AND PRESS RELEASES

Another form of marketing includes article writing, press releases, guest posting, and video blogging. Consider attending local group events to link up with blog writers and journalists to see if there is an opportunity for you to work together. By attending these events and getting to know local writers, you can build a list of contacts for both writing and distributing your content. You can also find local groups using many resources including Meetup.com, BNI, conferences, trade shows, and by simply asking friends and colleagues for suggestions. In addition to local distribution methods, you should look to distribute your releases within e-mail newsletters, RSS feeds, and using social media networks. Your business should not only release news of big events and happenings within the company, but should also share stories of awards, conferences, products, and other unique marketplace events and activities.

# CHAPTER 5

# Making Dollars With Sense

## SELLING VALUE

### GAINING ATTENTION

Cost leadership is a term used to describe a strategic concept that entails creating a competitive advantage in a business/sales market by producing a quality product or service at a better value compared to the competition. Although *cost* is in the name, value is the major factor in cost leadership. The quality of your product or service may influence your overall value and increase or lower the cost at which you sell your products or services. You don't always have to sell at the lowest price or match prices, but you should offer competitive prices and value that is beneficial to both the business and the targeted consumer. Most industries are polluted with low-cost and cheap alternatives, so it may be difficult for customers to understand why you don't lower your price. Your marketing materials and your staff will need to get across to your customers that you offer a better service than your competition. For example, relay to customers that your product is backed by services that add value to the product such as expert advice and dedicated personnel, bundling capabilities, frequent-buyer rewards programs, and education. Base your marketing on understanding the customer's needs, and adapt and sell toward that point. For instance, a customer who wants to keep costs down is unlikely to select an expensive company to purchase from. For customers seeking quality results, you should focus your sales pitch on your strengths by providing examples, references, and knowledge.

Some methods for influencing customers to purchase include:

- Persuade buyers they will achieve worthwhile results.
- Minimize the perception of risk by demonstrating experience, building trust, and inspiring confidence.
- Connect with customers by listening to, and addressing, their needs and desires from your business.

The difficulty of gaining the attention of customers is not whether you are competitive, but how well you know your customers. Trying to please everyone is a difficult task. Your prices will never be cheap enough, and your quality will never satisfy all customers. By focusing your attention on your key customer demographics, you can put together a competitive package at an affordable price for your desired customer group.

## SELL WHAT SELLS

The goal of any campaign is to generate sales. Therefore, the ideal campaign should build trust, influence sales, and generate brand awareness. The trick to selling is to give customers what they want or something better. As a business, you need to focus your marketing campaigns on the services or products which have proven to generate sales. Your business should target and adapt your marketing strategies to highlight what customers want and will purchase, not necessarily what you want to sell. For example, if Product A (the product you least like) sells more than Product B (the product you want to sell), then you need to adjust your business and focus on the product that is generating a profit and sustaining your business.

When I started as a consultant, I worked under the business name Tex Design Studio (TDS) where I worked directly with customers to sell web design, SEO, marketing, and other services which I outsourced to artists and developers. After a few years, I had discovered that my TDS brand was not growing as I would have liked. Customers were calling the business for me, and me only. They were also Googling my name and referring me any not my company to their family and friends. Considering this, I realized I had been trying to push a brand on customers that they did not want. I wanted so badly to grow the company, that I made it difficult for those customers who wanted something entirely different. As I realized this and adjusted to the customers, I stopped pushing TDS and gave the customers the personal brand that they wanted by renaming my consulting agency Elijah Clark and Associates which proved to be much more successful than TDS ever was or could have been.

The customer is the ultimate power broker within any organization. And as the power brokers, they will set your selling price, name (or rename) your business, help you decide which products to sell, and let you know when it's time to hire or fire employees. Because of the authority in which customers have on the success of your business, you should structure your marketing efforts on identifying and meeting the customer's individual needs. Those needs must be met within all aspects of your business including price, customer support, and overall value.

## THE TRIGGER POINT

While working on my bachelor degree, I was employed as a student recruiter for a local college in Dallas, Texas. During sales training, I learned lessons that remain current in all my customer relationships: Never ruin a hot lead and know the customer's trigger point. Finding the trigger point is as simple as asking "Why are you calling or meeting with me today?" Every customer has a reason for the decision to do business with you, at your particular location, with your price, and on that singular day. In education, reasons adult students chose to go back to school included that they wanted to do it for their family or kids, they wanted to change the world, or they wanted to go to school to prove to someone who said or believed they couldn't achieve a higher education.

In relationships, you wouldn't marry someone you just met. You date for a short while and get to know their likes, dislikes, and interests. It's the same with customers. When you have found the customer's decision-making trigger, you can easily put together a strategy that helps you get to the next stage of satisfying them. The goal of sales is to find and finesse your customers' trigger point. If a customer wants to purchase your product or service because it would make them more productive, it is your responsibility to continually integrate that *productivity* trigger in conversations by noting how your product or service could help with their productivity. Once the trigger point is outlined, the sale becomes much easier. Your customer has a reason for doing business with you, and it is your responsibility to figure out what that reason is and make that trigger point your key to developing a successful selling strategy.

## BEING DIFFERENT

You can overcome your competition by offering products or

services that are unique to your industry. When attempting to set your business apart from the rest with a unique product or service, you may arrive at situations where your customer does not fully understand your unique benefits. You will need to educate your customers on why your product or service is better for their personal or business needs.

A potential setback of creating differentiators such as unique features, services, and benefits, is that you are open to imitation by your competition if your differentiators are not proprietary. In this sense, your uniqueness will last only as long as it takes your competition to mimic your approach. Additionally, by offering too many differentiators or products, your customers could become confused, overwhelmed, or feel that you're trying to sell them something they don't need. To resolve this, take precautions and carefully educate your customers on the offerings and the importance and relevancy of the additional products or services.

**Value Proposition.** Customers have more options at their disposal than ever before, with that in mind, a well-drafted value proposition should be at the core of your sales collateral to solidify your competitive advantage. A value proposition is a statement of promise in terms of overall value delivered to the customer, and is a major factor in increasing sales. A value proposition helps you define how your product is the better solution for your customers' needs. A strong value proposition is persuasive and outlines why the customer should purchase your product or service over the competition.

Having an effective and unique value proposition (UVP) is of critical importance as it distinguishes your business from your competitors. A UVP should uniquely identify the value of your business and should resonate strongly with your customers. For example, if you offer a product or service for the price of $10, and your competitor offers the same product or service for $11, what stops your competitor from stealing your customer if they match or lower their price? While price is considered a UVP, unless it is tremendously lower than the competition, you need to offer better and more UVPs.

UVPs may include:

- Better price point
- Better product quality
- Better location
- Better customer service / hours
- Better warranty / guarantee

Your business can evaluate and enhance customer benefits through gaining feedback from reviews of current, previous, and potential customers. Through this method, flaws within your business can be identified and needed corrections made. Another valuable method is to monitor your competitors' marketing efforts, as well as gain insight into your reputation, by reviewing forums, complaint boards, and competitor websites for credibility, design, and customer testimonials.

## PRICING

Setting and presenting your price may be the single most important thing to get right in your business. When determining the value of your product or service, keep in mind that pricing low will lower your revenue, introduce a new lower quality customer, and could damage the growth of your business. Low pricing also creates low motivation from you or your team and will often prevent you from going the extra mile for the customer. However, pricing high may give your competition the upper-hand with customers looking to spend less.

**How to Price.** You should set your price based on the true value of the product or service, which, in addition to the cost of producing any tangible product, includes the cost to cover the tools, software, electricity, employees, etc. In addition, the cost should easily allow you to reach your break-even point. The goal of your price should be to generate sales in excess of 50% above the break-even mark. Never make it a habit of charging your customers based on your lack of knowledge or technology. Your customer should never pay because you don't know how to do your job properly or efficiently. However, if the customer has a unique problem that involves research and no easy solution, which may include a system hack, training, or simply writing a document or tutorial, you should charge based on the time it takes you to research and resolve the issue. Your customers should not be concerned with the time it takes for you to complete their request. They care about the value you bring. If they believe that you are the best, then your price may not be relevant. If you have tough competition and the customer doesn't care about the quality you bring, then the price is very important and you will need to also consider the competition and brand reputation when setting prices.

**Real vs. Perceived Value.** Value pricing attracts value conscious customers. The actual cost of product production determines the real value. In addition, the real value is dependent on the usefulness of the product to the customer as well as the value of the product components. Ultimately, the perceived value is based on how much money the customer believes the product is worth.

For example, in the context of higher education, the perceived value of a college or university among individuals looking to invest in higher education tremendously affects the institution's price. Students and their families perceive the value of the institution to be within the quality of the education. Consequently, the higher the perceived value of quality, the higher the cost of tuition. Research, however, has not proven correlation between institutional cost and actual quality.

Additionally, it was found that perceived value of an institution did correlate with a student's likelihood of enrollment. Perceived value of an education has three main factors which include, quality, cost, and emotional attachment. Failing to satisfy either of these could jeopardize the student's enrollment potential as it will affect the student's perceived value. In marketing, generating excitement can also generate a sale and loyal customers. If a customer is excited about a product, they may ignore the cost and quality factor. If an individual truly believes in the quality and value of a product or service, then the perceived value becomes more valuable than the real value.

# CHAPTER 6

# Attracting The Right Attention

# MARKETING AND ADVERTISING

## PURPOSE OF MARKETING

Without marketing, your business is taking the risk of losing customers and revenue. Think of your brand, website, or artwork as a resume. You spend hours or days writing, designing, and editing it to perfection, not to mention the years of enhancing and refining your background with experience and education. After you've culminated and perfected your resume, what next? What's the next step to ensuring that you land that dream job? The appropriate response is to send your resume to employers. In the context of business, that's called marketing. You must market yourself to win the job. A terribly unattractive resume sent to potential employers has a higher probability of landing a job over a superb resume sitting in a drawer. Without marketing, you will waste time and money creating a great brand that never gets noticed.

## CUSTOMER MARKETING

If your marketing strategy is not structured on the purchasing needs and wants of your desired customer, you are missing the *mark* in marketing. An effective campaign is one that influences customers to make a purchase. The secret is to build trust and positive brand awareness through attractive and targeted marketing. Additionally, the campaign should aim at solving the customer's hesitation to purchase. As customers make purchases, a trend will develop, outlining likes and dislikes based on what sells and what doesn't.

**A Hesitant Customer.** All customers experience some hesitancy before making purchases. They don't simply walk into a store or view a website and make a purchase without thinking about it. How long they hesitate is where you should focus your marketing. For example, a product discounted with a "One day only" stamp will make the customer spend less time debating the purchase because of the urgency of the deadline. If you want a *today* purchase, you should try marketing your product or service so that it positively influences the customer to decide and act quickly.

As a business owner, you have the responsibility to provide customers with the information they need to make a purchase. If presented effectively, the information you provide customers can persuade them to believe they need what your business is selling, even if the product is outside of their immediate desires or needs. In this sense, information used within your marketing efforts are responsible for shaping the needs and wants of your customers. The implication is that, through marketing, you can capitalize on your customers' internal weakness and persuade them to make a purchase.

A customer purchase is often based on one of three factors; (1) whether the product or service will help the customer be more productive; (2) whether the product or service can satisfy the things or people the customer cares most about; or (3) whether it fulfills a desire or need.

When marketing, you should understand how your product can solve your customers' problem or situation. If you know your customers' habits, likes, or dislikes you can market based on how your product will fit into their lifestyles. From there, the customer will be less hesitant to make the purchase and will have a solid answer as to why they *need* your product.

## CONSUMER VS BUSINESS MARKETS

In both business and consumer markets, the individual that will use your product or service is not always the same individual that makes the actual purchasing decision. For instance, a husband may purchase a product that his wife needs, or a parent for a child, or an employer for an employee. In these situations, your responsibility is to satisfy the decision maker(s) by providing them relevant information as to how your product or service can enhance their business or lifestyle.

Generally, when I walk into a jewelry store to purchase a gift for my wife, the sales representative will ask questions about my wife, not about me (until we start talking budget). In business, you need to ask the purchaser about the goals or intentions for the product or service, not about *their* basic needs. To make *them* happy, you have to sell the expectation that the individual receiving the purchase will be happy. When the decision maker is not present, you can generate more sales by focusing on expectation rather than the moment.

**Business Market Purchases.** When marketing to a business, you should concentrate on what is most important to the business which often includes statistics, facts, data, and a return on investment. Within the business market, the purchasing decision is generally made by multiple individuals. Your selling strategy should focus on each of the decision makers by way of the individual who sought out your business. This may include giving everything to the purchaser and letting that individual determine how to disperse the content to the decision maker(s).

**Consumer Market Purchases**. Consumers regularly make purchases based on factors which include value, availability, and emotional connections. In consumer markets, you will either sell to an individual or a couple. An example of a *couple* transaction is a husband wanting to purchase a new home. To do so, he would need to get his wife to agree to the decision. Similar to a business market, you need to sell to both but primarily satisfy the decision maker, which you should identify as you work to develop the relationship.

In both business and consumer markets, you can go a long way by getting the individual who contacted you to like you. If they like you and your business, they will fight on your behalf to influence the decision maker.

## MARKETING AUDIT

Based on questionnaires obtained by the opinions of marketing experts, it has been determined that marketing audits are a paramount factor in business success.[9] A marketing audit can be an important tool in discovering potential risks within your business's activities. Within the marketing industry, understanding how or why to market to a certain demographic is a key component to creating a successful marketing plan. To

---

[9] Lipnická D., Ďaďo J. (2013). Marketing Audit and Factors Influencing Its Use in Practice of Companies (From an Expert Point of View). Journal of Competitiveness, 5 (4), 26-42. doi: 10.7441/joc.2013.04.02

conduct an effective marketing audit, the method should have four major characteristics which include it being comprehensive regarding function, environment, and productivity; independent from decision-making managers; completed using a structured, systematic approach; and that it should be carried out on a periodic basis. A marketing audit can improve your marketing management and business problems by helping to assess and evaluate your business's marketing ability, strategies, performance and effectiveness, problematic areas, and opportunities.

Having the ability to find and understand your customer, competitor, and product potential will make the process of marketing your product or service much easier. A problem often found in businesses is that they don't develop marketing strategies or perform preemptive audits. These businesses come to realize, in the middle of their marketing efforts, that they have no real plan or a way to monitor the effects of their marketing campaigns. Having a plan of action serves to pace and organize your marketing efforts. Regular audits can help you identify business strengths, weaknesses, opportunities, and risks specific to your industry and market. Furthermore, marketing audits can be used to direct the vision of your business, the value of products offered, and the effectiveness of current, previous, and future marketing efforts and organizational efficiencies. A good marketing audit should also assist with the implementation of a marketing strategy, and help in generating brand awareness and sales.

## MARKETING STRATEGY

Marketing plans are crucial for starting and growing your business. A good marketing plan will help your business identify target customers and generate a plan to reach and retain those customers. The marketing plan can be a roadmap to gaining customers and improving organizational success if done properly. Additionally, this strategy can help to define your desired customer by targeting their precise needs based on their demographic profiles which are helpful in identifying targeted customers and creating focused advertisements aimed directly at those prospective customers.

**Strategy Development.** Carefully developing your marketing strategy and performance will help keep your market presence strong. Without planning, you could potentially waste time and money targeting the wrong audience. Effective marketing is often based on the importance of how your customers perceive your business, and has two important principles:

- Your business policies and activities should be directed toward satisfying customer needs.
- Profitable sales volume is more important than maximum sales volume.

There is no one method of creating a flawless marketing plan. The most effective tried and true method is taking the time to do the necessary research and stay updated on your market and target consumer groups. Monitoring population shifts, legal developments, and local economic situations can help to identify problems and discover opportunities for your business. Monitoring your competitors' successes and failures is also helpful in devising your marketing strategies.

**Strategy Implementation.** To develop a successful business, create a strategy that can be followed for implementing the plan. Marketing implementation is the process that ensures the strategy accomplishes its stated objectives. For instance, if the plan refers to building search engine optimization, it should also mention which keywords to optimize for and why those keywords are best suited for the task. The plan should mention why following the planned strategy will be effective at producing positive results. Furthermore, the plan should include an analysis of the competition and market potential.

**Marketing Message.** The marketing message is the heart of a marketing plan. It details the business' plan for the marketing materials, how the company plans to achieve its marketing goals and the tactics that will be used to meet them. In addition, the marketing message determines how your business intends to communicate its message to customers. When creating your marketing message, make certain that you focus on how you want your company to be perceived by its customers. Do you want customers to view your business as having good prices, customer support, or quality service? Once you determine your marketing message, you will know the next steps to take for your business.

**Marketing Plan vs Business Plan**. Marketing plans are the starting points for successful businesses, and the plan often includes dozens to hundreds of pages worth of data analysis. The difference between a marketing plan and a business plan is that a **business plan** focuses mainly on defining the company in terms of its history, mission, and goals. In addition, a business plan includes details regarding staffing, locations, finances, and strategic alliances. A **marketing plan** focuses on creating keys to success by telling the story of how you plan to achieve your business goals and generate success.

Business and marketing plans are best when there are many people involved in its creation. Each of the business's leaders and managers should assist with the creation of the plan and give insight into whether the plan is achievable. Gaining feedback is also important considering most ideas will affect each department within the company. Leaders and managers can provide realistic data, experiences, and share insight into business and marketing opportunities.

**Analyzing a Marketing Plan**. Your marketing plan should include everything from understanding the desired customer to determining how to outperform and strategize the competition. A plan is paramount to achieving business success and the time taken to develop a marketing plan is an investment worth making. The goal of a strategic marketing plan is to direct and coordinate your marketing efforts. The salient features of a marketing plan include goals and objectives and should address the who, where, when, and how of a marketing goal.

The levels in which a marketing plan operates are strategic and tactical. **Strategic** levels focus on the target market and the company's value proposition. **Tactical** level marketing plans specify marketing tactics such as product features, promotions, pricing, sales channels, and services.

**Distribution**. A critical point of your marketing plan is its plan of distribution. The distribution plan details the channels and processes through which customers can make purchases and how your business will reach new customers. The distribution strategy of the plan is considered one of the most important sections of the plan. Examples of an effective distribution strategy include tactics utilizing television, trade shows, and online advertising.

**Strategy Milestones** cover the business' major events and achievements that need to occur to keep your strategy on track for success. Milestone events are strategically important for your business and provide an outline of dates and timeframes as to when the events should take place. Additionally, the milestones should be tracked and analyzed with real results. Not sticking to the plan and milestones will likely cause your strategy to fail, particularly, in reaching its expected completion date.

# MARKETING RESEARCH

It is difficult to be both a specialist in your profession and an expert in understanding your current and potential customers. If your expertise is in being a chef or hair stylist, you shouldn't expect to launch a top-notch website or marketing campaign using analytics, data analysis, or customer insight without actually taking the time to understand marketing research in the same way that you learned your profession. In developing marketing strategies and enhancing your knowledge, it is essential to conduct market research to better comprehend your customer base and their needs. Like any profession, effective marketing requires time and dedication to gain the experience necessary to properly research and analyze your customers, considering they do not always think, act, believe, or have the same priorities or values as you. The keys to understanding how to grow your business are in researching your industry and target consumer group. Once you have researched your customers and analyzed the data, you need to develop a targeted strategy to grow sales. Only then will your marketing efforts and business flourish.

## MARKET RESEARCH METHODS

Marketing research knowledge has significantly increased in response to growth in disruptive innovations including the internet and technology development. In my experience, I have found that market research has been essential when repositioning my business to support product advancement, and in helping discover marketing opportunities and expanding market shares through various conveyance channels. Additionally, marketing research has helped influence the performance and effectiveness of my marketing strategies by helping to find my ideal customer with little error and without wasting time and resources on customers that were never going to purchase.

To help with analyzing markets, there are two useful forms of marketing research; primary and secondary.

**Primary Research**. This is a research methodology where you interact with your customers and gather as much information as you can directly from them. The information is generally collected through surveys, questionnaires, feedback forms, and interviews.

**Secondary Research**. This research relies on information which has been collected by others (blogs, previous researchers, data channels). You should conduct this type of research by collecting and analyzing articles, web pages, and books as references for the collected research data.

**Phenomenology**. A phenomenology research method uses analysis to capture individual customer experiences. This method is used for unfolding customer experiences by examining the uniqueness and commonalities of events and circumstances. The data collection techniques used in phenomenology research include in-depth analysis, documentary, and observation.

## Quantitative, Qualitative, and Mixed Methods

When conducting research, you should first decide the method of research you intend to use. Research study methodologies are characterized as either qualitative, quantitative, or a combination of both, which is referred to as mixed methods. Of these methods, none can be considered the best method without factoring in the goals and objectives of your research.

I know it may seem a bit overwhelming, but understanding research methods are critical if you desire a certain outcome for your marketing efforts. For example, when I'm putting together an AdWords campaign, I would rather put together my campaign based on data collected from a quantitative method versus a qualitative method. Otherwise, I would waste time and money guessing what to do based on trial and error. A quantitative research method is better for helping to pinpoint your customer and develop a more effective marketing campaign.

**Quantitative.** A quantitative research method is beneficial for collecting data in the form of tests, reliance, probability theory, and surveys for analyzing statistical hypotheses that relate to your business, marketing goal, or research questions. A quantitative research method is best used when you want to analyze numbers. For example, you could use a quantitative approach when sending out a survey where you expect to get the survey results in numerical format, or if the survey has multiple choice questions.

**Qualitative.** Qualitative research consists of using real-world experiences and interpreting the phenomena. Unlike quantitative research, a qualitative examination is non-measurable. This research method can be used to help you understand and discover experiences, perspectives, and insight of your customers. An advantage of a qualitative approach is that the study participants are not constrained to a predetermined set of responses such as those in multiple choice or numerical questions. Meaning, through qualitative research, the participants would give their broad perception versus clicking a checkbox or radio button like in surveys.

Unlike a quantitative method, a qualitative examination technique can help to assess why customers behave a certain way. The method also helps in discovering boundaries that influence thought by breaking down points of interest and gathering information from in-depth sources. A quantitative method often makes the assumption that there is a singular truth that exists, which does not include human perception. A drawback of using a quantitative approach to collect data is that it is expensive considering the amount of time needed to collect and analyze the data.

**Mixed Methods.** Mixed methods are useful when you want to combine qualitative and quantitative methods by linking their differences. The key principle of mixed methods is that various forms of data can be collected by using multiple strategies and methods. Mixed methods can assist in reflecting complementary strengths and weaknesses of qualitative and quantitative methods, and produce opportunities for approaches with weaknesses by correcting method biases.

Determining whether to use a qualitative or quantitative method is dependent upon the importance of how you desire to collect your data. Simply stated, qualitative techniques define and describe while quantitative techniques estimate and quantify. When creating a new marketing strategy, neither qualitative nor quantitative measures are more important than the other when determining value and sales. If you are confused on which method to use, testing both measures will help you find the best outcomes.

# DATA MINING AND PROCESSING

You can develop business and marketing strategies by analyzing customer patterns and behaviors. In a U.S. study, it was found that 93% of customers use the internet for e-commerce-related activities.[10] In addition to general data mining using the internet, social media was also useful for gathering location-based data about customers and identifying patterns of consumer feedback. Other data mining sources include weblogs, forums, wikis, and social media.

Comprehending the needs of your customers can help to establish future direction and define your product status.

---

[10] Flanagin, A. J., Metzger, M. J., Pure, R., Markov, A., & Hartsell, E. (2014). Mitigating risk in ecommerce transactions: Perceptions of information credibility and the role of user-generated ratings in product quality and purchase intention. Electronic Commerce Research, 14, 1-23. doi:10.1007/s10660-014-9139-2

Additionally, online data mining from social media networks is advantageous for gathering data quicker and easier than surveys and questionnaires. Benefits of data mining include the capacity to better comprehend your customers by knowing and assessing the networks in which they gather. Moreover, data mining is useful for analyzing customer behavior, which can assist in establishing a future course for identifying and implementing your business's marketing strategies.

## PERSONAL LEARNING NETWORK

Another method used for gaining customer insight is to develop a personal learning network (PLN). The network may consist of a few friends or individuals you know that can assist in providing honest feedback for the purpose of data collection. With so many opportunities to develop skills and knowledge, having a PLN is essential to advancing and strengthening one's understanding and education. Having a PLN is important because it is an opportunity to connect with individuals or businesses that can help you in developing insight and provide a difference in professional opinion. Through a PLN connection, you can get answers to questions and take advantage of opportunities provided by those within your PLN. Through these networks, professionals within a PLN can share personal and professional ideas through short status updates, blogs, photos, and videos. This information can be used as resources to help develop your brand or marketing message.

## FOCUS GROUPS

Qualitative research focuses on analyzing the in-depth details of why customers behave the way in which they do. It searches for the barriers in place that may affect a customer's reasoning. For instance, a new company may want to know about their product in terms of how it feels, smells, and tastes. Using a qualitative approach would assist in finding the appropriate marketing or product solution. A qualitative research setting would be used to collect user information and explore the reasoning for their perspectives. In addition to those responses, details could be collected to determine how they arrived at their conclusions. Those details could include motives, emotions, and mental triggers. A focus group setting would be perfect for conducting qualitative research considering that focus groups allow for in-depth interviews with customers that can be used to gain valuable product insight.

Focus groups can provide your business with resources to seek legitimate feedback, conduct beta testing, and evaluate customers' perceptions through real-time reviews. Focus groups are ideal for acquiring data for measuring status and trends while also providing your business the opportunity to decide the cost of products and services based on the opinion of topographically diverse participants. The core segment of focus groups are the connections among the participants. In particular, the interaction with participants could help gather less accessible data, which would not generally come to surface using traditional data collection methods. Focus groups are also more reliable than data mining on social media because of careful validation processes that consider time, commitment, and credibility of the results produced by study participants.

The drawbacks of using focus groups are that using the method would not help you observe participants in a natural setting, which often affect the results. However, in an attempt to analyze the reliability of focus groups, researchers concluded that the group setting was as reliable as other methods of interviews, and the credibility relied on the mentalities and demographics of participants. Considering focus groups take place within a group setting, participants could affect the decisions of other individuals. Therefore, using a structured process is critical to the success of focus groups.

# CHAPTER 7

## Data Does Not Lie

# MARKETING CAMPAIGNS

### CALL-TO-ACTION

Once you start delivering amazing experiences to your website's anonymous visitors, you'll want to learn more about those visitors so you can create personalized and targeted messaging and content. To do that, you'll need two key ingredients: A call-to-action (CTA) and a landing page. A CTA is an image or line of text that prompts your visitors, leads, and customers to take action. It is, quite literally, a "call" to take an "action."

CTAs should entice your visitors to want to learn more about a particular topic and then lead those visitors to a landing page where they can schedule a consultation, download content, or submit a form. In exchange for downloaded content, visitors fill out a form with their name, email address, and other information. A great place to use CTAs is on your blog. The objective here is to align the messaging of your CTA with the content of the blog post on which your CTA is appearing. If, for example, a visitor is reading a blog post on cats and dogs, don't show them a CTA promoting an eBook about marketing automation. Instead, show them a CTA promoting an eBook (or other type of content) about cats and dogs!

It sounds simple, but overlooking the alignment between your website's content and the CTA can mean the difference between a visitor who feels like you're catering to their interests and a visitor who feels like you don't understand them at all. Once anonymous visitors submit a form on a landing page (or on a form embedded elsewhere on your site), you'll be able to use the information they submit to refine your landing page so they are more personalized.

The action you want customers to take could be anything: Download an eBook, sign up for a webinar, get a coupon, attend an event, etc. A CTA can be placed anywhere in your marketing process including your website, in an eBook, in an email, or even at the end of a blog post. But here's the catch with getting started with CTAs: You can't just slap "Click Here!" on a neon button, insert it on your website, and start raking in the clicks and leads. There are several crucial elements you need to include in a CTA if you want to entice people to actually take an action. A CTA won't always be to purchase your product or service. It can certainly lead people in that direction, but it will rarely follow as a direct result of an isolated marketing tactic.

## COST PER CLICK

Google's Ad Rank program is designed to help you display the most relevant ad content to your customers and to provide an equal system that benefits both the customer and your business. The Ad Rank system is controlled by your ad quality, which is determined by the websites click through rate (CTR) and ad relevance to landing page content and keywords used. Ad Rank works by helping customers gain satisfaction through seeing more relevant ads to their keyword, and you get to show more relevant ads for your product or service so that you attract the right customer group. The result is that your business gains satisfied and relevant customers. Additionally, Ad Rank is used to determine where (and if) your ads appear and how much you pay each time a user clicks on your ad. The ranking system is created using a mathematical formula that decides which ads appear within the top positions of Google's AdWords.

A cost-per-click (**CPC**) is the amount you choose or agree to pay each time a potential customer clicks on your Google ad in AdWords. A **Quality Score** is a numerical estimate based on the overall combined quality of your ads, keywords, and landing pages. The formula used to create your Ad Rank is: Ad Rank = Max CPC x Quality Score.

*Example Case Study.* Mike's Biscuits (MB) has a current quality score of 3 for the keyword "Dog Biscuits." To find the Ad Rank position, MB can calculate the Max CPC ($4) by the Quality Score (3), and the result equals 12. If MB raises its quality score to at least a 7, the company could easily lower its CPC to $2 and end with an overall rank of 14. With a higher quality score, MB can pay half the cost and rank higher than with its lower quality score of 3 and budget of $4. To raise its Ad Rank position, MB should focus on raising its quality score by increasing its click-through-rate (CTR), keyword relevancy to users' search query's, and by creating an optimized landing page that holds original relevant content. The higher the quality score, the lower the CPC. Ultimately, the Google quality score system allows for the prevention of advertisers to pay their way to the top of the search results within Google's search engine. With this system, the higher quality score will save the advertiser money, create better placement, and increase the business's revenue.

## COST PER ACQUISITION

Cost per acquisition is more than just a way to measure your search market advertising. It's also a means to assess your multi-channel marketing and customer acquisition equity. Customer acquisition equity rivals return on investment (ROI), and by understanding ROI, your marketing communication achieves optimization.

- Cost Per Acquisition = Total Advertising Cost/Number of Total Leads
- ROI = (Revenue - Total Adverting Cost)/Total Advertising Cost

Tracking campaign channels is key to creating and understanding marketing and customer acquisition. Let's say you're a business with no prior marketing background wanting to gain new customers, you need to:

- Have an online presence for your brand.
- Optimize your website.
- Outline true costs associated for your marketing campaigns.
- Establish marketing campaign goals.
- Set a realistic cost you are willing to spend for each new customer lead.
- Align your marketing to your website.
- Focus your marketing directly at your intended target audience.

*Example*:

If you ran a three-month Valpak ad, which specifies an expiry date and has a total advertising costs of $2,000, and you're willing to pay $15 for each new potential customer, your ad would need to produce at least 133 potential leads to break-even. To illustrate why you need to be realistic with your budget, consider your projected revenue return. Let's say you're selling bags of crushed rocks for $55, with a goal of selling 133 bags. However, you only have two leads that purchase a total of 10 bags each. With only 20 of 133 sold, your ROI is -84.96%.

Now let's examine the same example, but instead you advertise in AdWords using an optimized landing page with a downloadable coupon as well as a mobile coupon that specifies an expiry date. Your total advertising costs are $2000 over a three-month period, and you had 500 potential new customers view your deal. At the end of the expiry date, you capitalize from 200 customers who purchased a total of 2000 bags of crush rock at $55/bag.

- Your CPA = $4, and your ROI = 5400%
- What's even better, is that you use your Web Analytics to:
    - Drive down future CPA
    - Increase ROI
    - Optimize your marketing

Now that's power in understanding your marketing measure, retention cost, and future revenue transactions as well as realization of the importance of customer acquisition equity for how to best allocate your advertising pay-out mix.

## A/B TESTING

When developing marketing campaigns, you should always A/B Test, which is referred to as creating multiple campaigns for the same goal. By creating multiple versions of a controlled campaign, it could help your business determine the most effective campaign based on a side-by-side comparison.

*Example.*

In a study conducted by the Coca-Cola Company, taste was considered the most important factor for their declined sales between the 1970s and 1980s. In response, the New Coke was developed to enhance the flavor and generate sales. With the approval of more than half of the 200,000 blind product testers, the New Coke was introduced to replace the original flavored Coke— which was a disaster for the company. Because of the unfavorable results and backlash from customers, the New Coke was withdrawn from the market and the Coke Classic was introduced with the original ingredients. Regarding the Coca-Cola Company's quantitative study and the New Coke, the test provided inconclusive results because of the lack of information given to the participants. Though the participants enjoyed the flavor of the New Coke, it did not outweigh their desire and loyalty of the original Coke. The New Coke's example of relying on only one type of study displayed poor predictive validity. A customer's like toward a product is not a good predictor of whether they would purchase the product over another product they also like. Had the Coke Company taken a segmented approach and kept both products on the store shelves, they could have had a better idea of which the users liked best and which would generate the most sales in a side-by-side or A/B comparison.

Most businesses who do A/B testing often fail to give their testing ad a chance at achieving its best possible results. Furthermore, without testing the ad properly, these individuals or companies may ultimately lose money, time, and potentially reject a successful ad that just never had the chance to prove itself successful due to the lack of owner knowledge. Having a control ad running throughout the testing of a new ad can save money and eliminate performance history as a variable in the test ad. By creating multiple copies of a control ad, you can avoid giving 50% of impressions to an unproven ad which may fail. Creating multiple copies of a control ad allows you to save on cost considering the control ad is always running. Instead of losing 50% of ad impressions to the testing ad, that percentage shrinks to 20% because of the additional control ad copies. In addition to this type of testing saving on cost and potentially accelerating the testing process, it also allows for you to create a valid testing environment by comparing the performance of the test ad against the copies of the control only.

## CUSTOMER PERSONA

In advertising, there are four user personas identified as competitive, spontaneous, humanistic, and methodical. The goal of a marketing campaign is to develop strategies for each persona, or to retain your preferred user persona and market toward only that group. Individuals within groups react differently to campaigns. Consequently, you should develop your campaigns to attract your desired customers using various strategies which include specific elements:

- Competitive - logical, quick (fast)
- Spontaneous - emotional, quick
- Methodical - deliberate, logical
- Humanistic - emotional, deliberate (slow)

**Competitive.** The competitive customer is business minded, power oriented, and does not like to waste time. This customer looks for businesses that have high qualifications, a positive track record, and a stellar reputation. This customer reacts strongly to marketing campaigns that outline what you can do for them and how you will support their ideas and conclusions. The best marketing strategy for this customer is to provide them with options, probabilities, and better results than they've previously enjoyed from other businesses.

Questions the Competitive customer considers when purchasing:

- What are your competitive advantages?
- Why are you a superior choice?
- Are you a credible company?
- How can you help me be more productive?
- How can you help me look good?
- What are your credentials?
- How can you help me achieve my goals?

**Spontaneous.** The spontaneous persona enjoys marketing campaigns that are personalized and activity oriented. This customer requires you to present evidence that you are trustworthy and customer service oriented. In marketing to this demographic, you will need to present evidence showcasing why your business is the best solution for them. You can achieve results by focusing on their feelings, interest, and excitement. Additionally, you can help them select your business by offering guarantees and recommendations, but not options.

Questions the Spontaneous customer considers when purchasing:

- How can you quickly get me what I need?
- Do you offer superior service?
- Can I customize your product or service?
- Can you help me narrow down my choices?
- How quickly can I take action and achieve my goals?
- How will your product/service help me enjoy life more?

**Humanistic.** The humanistic customer reacts to personal and relationship-driven campaigns. This type of customer is somewhat slower in making decisions and desires to develop a personal relationship with you and your business. Their decisions are primarily based on who you are, what you know, and how well you know them, their business, and their market. You can attract this customer using testimonials and a highly attractive portfolio.

Questions the Humanistic customer considers when purchasing:

- How will your product or service make me feel?
- Who uses your products/services?
- Who are you? Tell me who your company is and let me see bios.
- What will it feel like to work with you?
- What experience have others had with you?
- Can I trust you?
- What are your business values?

**Methodical.** The methodical customer is detail oriented and disciplined with their time. This customer will require evidence of your experience, processes, and knowledge. The desire of this customer is for you to prove that you can provide solutions. You can attract this customer by offering a solution that is rational and supports their principles.

Questions the Methodical customer considers when purchasing:

- What are the details of your offering, including the fine print?
- What processes will you use?
- Can you take me through the process step-by-step?
- What are the product specs?
- What proof do you have that you can help me?
- Can you guarantee your product or work?

*Example campaigns for a marketing agency.*

**Competitive**: *Professional Marketing Services. Beat out your competition. Build a successful online brand.* The competitive persona looks for a company that has a positive and successful reputation. This ad would satisfy the competitive persona looking for marketing services as it showcases a professional agency that knows how to help them get to the top of their industry.

**Humanistic**: *Affordable Marketing. Stay connected with your customers. We have a plan to help you succeed.* This ad will be great for the humanistic persona as it explains to them that they will be able to stay connected with their customers, which they would desire to do so. It also shows that they can contact the agency who will develop a personalized plan for success.

**Methodical**: *Professional Marketing. Proven success stories. 100% Satisfaction Guaranteed.* This headline will draw in the methodical personality because it shows that it's not a freelance or amateur company, which methodical customers generally do not prefer. Providing money back will also provide further proof that the agency is trustworthy and customer friendly.

**Spontaneous**: *Affordable Marketing Offer! Low-cost marketing services. Get started on your marketing TODAY!* This headline can be used to draw in the spontaneous persona, as they are normally looking for easy, fast, and affordable.

## EFFECTIVE CAMPAIGN HEADLINES

In a study conducted by HubSpot, it was discovered that the word, "tip" decreased customer click-through-rates (CTR) by 59% when used in campaign headlines and descriptions. Headlines with the word "easy" generated a 44% lower CTR than headlines without this word. There was a 49% decrease in CTR among headlines containing the word "simple." Headlines that used the positive superlatives "always" or "best" performed 14% worse than headlines that did not. Headlines that made references to the reader by including the word, "you," "your," or "you're" performed 36% worse than headlines that did not contain any of these words. Headlines with language that conveys a sense of urgency ("need", "now") generated lower CTRs than headlines that didn't use such pushy language (44% and 12% lower).[11]

## EMAIL

When done correctly, email marketing serves as a tried-and-true way to get readers to download content, convert prospects with special offers, and upsell existing customers. It's important to focus your time and attention on email marketing in addition to social media, paid advertising, and search engine optimization. It's one form of marketing that's not going anywhere any time soon, and rightfully so.

With emails, you can foster a deeper, one-on-one relationship with your customers. Your emails have the opportunity to appear more personal and authentic than any other marketing effort. This builds trust with your customers considering the message creates (or appears to create) a one-on-one dialogue. Email subscribers are 3.9 times more likely to share content via the social web. Plus, your target audience wants to hear from you via email. It was discovered in a survey conducted by MarketingSherpa that 72% of people actually prefer to receive promotional content through email from businesses they like, as compared to the 17% who prefer social media.[12]

When sending email campaigns, make sure your strategy, and your business, answers questions such as:

---

[11] http://cdn2.hubspot.net/hub/53/file-2505556912-pdf/Data_Driven_Strategies_For_Writing_Effective_Titles_and_Headlines.pdf
[12] http://content.marketingsherpa.com/data/public/reports/benchmark-reports/EXCERPT-BMR-2013-Email-Marketing.pdf

- What are you trying to accomplish with the email?
- What actions do you want customers to take?
- How will you prompt customers to take this action (i.e., using buttons, CTAs, or by clearly spelling it out in the content of the email)?

Whether optimizing your email or just writing the content, you should always do so as if you were speaking directly to one person in your target audience. Use the same language in your email as you would if your ideal customer were standing in front of you. Speak (or in this case, write) to your one reader as if you already know them. This can be tricky at first, but it will get easier over time as you come to understand more about who your ideal customer is. One easy way to sound more conversational is to use second person pronouns — "you" and "your." This is a simple adjustment that makes the email about the reader, not your company.

**Personalize the Content.** In the same way that you personalized your subject line, you should also personalize the content within your email. According to research conducted by Aberdeen Group, personalized emails showed an increase in click-through rates of 14% and an increase in conversions by 10%. To get started with personalization, the simplest thing to do is address your recipients by their first name in your email greeting. Your customers will also appreciate your efforts since 74% of online customers get frustrated with websites when content (e.g., offers, ads, and promotions) appear to have nothing to do with their interests. [13]

**Newsletters** should be branded if you intend to share company news and not get lost amongst the spam. Temper the marketing tone of your messages by integrating stories about

---

[13] http://www.aberdeen.com/research/4904/ra-email-marketing/content.aspx

your staff and customers.

**Transactional emails** are emails that directly promote products, promotions, and include emails sent to confirm an order or new account sign-up. Keep these emails succinct, but write with flair.

**Videos** are a great way to bring your brand to life. They are the perfect vehicle to introduce your products and services. Be sure to keep them short and snappy, perfect for social media sharing.

**Business cards** are pocket-sized promotional opportunities. Make sure they include relevant details like your social media handles and links to your website. **Loyalty cards** are also good for encouraging return visits to your store and should reflect your brand. **Postcards** are a fun way to raise brand awareness. Whether you choose to mail them, add them to your packaging, or distribute them at local businesses, they must be attractive if you want customers to view and keep them.

Most agencies know how to leverage their own email marketing skills to attract and nurture new business. However, they often overlook email as a communication channel post-sale. Email can be used to entice your customers in a scalable way as it provides the means necessary to continuously deliver added value over the course of your relationship. While many would argue that no one is looking forward to more emails, your emails should be relevant and thoughtfully written to ensure you don't add to the SPAM issue.

**Customer Service.** These days, technology connects us in a way that we could have never imagined. And while this increased connectivity makes it easy for us to stay in touch, it's important that we don't let it stand in the way of real, personal engagement with customers. Think about a time when you called into a customer service line. You probably sat through a series of long, drawn-out automated messages, pressed a couple buttons, and after much frustration, breathed a sigh of relief when you were finally connected with an actual representative, right?

At the end of the day, people want to do business with other people — not machines and auto sequenced emails. By making a conscious effort to infuse more human interactions into your day-to-day communication with customers, it will be easier to build trust and deepen the relationship. Satisfying the needs of your customers ensures the survival of your business. A periodic check is required to discern the level of performance related to the current quality of services and products, followed by a plan to upgrade or enhance those services or products as necessary to build a quality relationship with your customers. In order to fulfill this goal, you must have a set of rules to measure and improve this quality.

Delivering quality services to customers is considered the most effective way to ensure that your business stands out from your competitors. The main ingredients involved in a quality relationship between your business and your customers are trust and commitment. Trust means confidence and security in the relationship you have with customers and can be treated as the biggest investment in building long term relationships. Lack of trust, on the other hand, weakens the relationship's foundation.

## ANALYTICS

Analytics are not necessarily about numbers, but about processes. It helps to evaluate what hinders people from getting from point A to point B. This starts with segmentation. Numbers don't show you the whole picture. Segmenting tells you the factors that lead to the actual data that you collect, which will then help you to adjust your strategy. Web analytics has many benefits. Some of these benefits include tracking website visits, hits, conversions, trends, ROI, goals, etc. With a web analytics solution, you can monitor:

- Where your site traffic is coming from.
- The IP addresses of your visitors.
- The customer's actions by sequence with a time stamp.

Analytics can also help measure:

- How many users visit your site, how many return, and how often.
- How users navigate through your website.
- Where in the "conversion funnel" or purchasing process customers are getting stuck and leaving.
- What content your visitors are looking for, and whether they're finding it.
- Exactly which form fields are driving people away rather than bringing them in.

With analytics, you can also monitor your visitors by seeing which browser type, operating system, and the originating country, state, and city from which they are visiting. This information is beneficial for creating an effective website and will help users gain the maximum experience while they are visiting your company site. With web analytics, being analytical is not enough, but it should also be combined with creativity and company knowledge. You may find that reading analytics is confusing, mostly because there is too much information to collect. As for where people originate from when they land on your website, there are many inlets. Trying to measure the effectiveness of each inlet is a daunting task, but worth the financial savings of having to market and research.

# TRACKING KPI'S

After reviewing your analytics report, you can confidently make a conclusion about your website's performance and identify actionable items that will help improve the key performance indicators (KPI) going forward. You can start by looking at the average time a user spends on your website. This report will be able to help measure how visitors interact with the website's content. If you dig deeper, you should be able to see which pages create the longest stay and conversions, and which pages users are not finding to be relevant toward their search. Digging even further, you can begin to see which pages users last visited before abandoning the website. If you see a common trend of user activity, you will be able to make the corrections as needed. The other two metrics, unique visitors and ratio of local audience to national audience, will be important in helping you understand how engaging your website content is to customers. These two metrics may also be useful in helping with future marketing. By having a true understanding of what your visitors are looking for, it will help you develop effective campaigns to accumulate more leads, which will lead to an increased ROI.

# CHAPTER **8**

# Always Be The Next Big Thing

## INTERNET AND SOCIAL TRENDS

### INTERNET TRENDS

The development of the internet has shifted businesses from paper-based and people-intensive purchasing frameworks toward electronic frameworks. In 2016, U.S. electronic commerce transactions accounted for $394.86 billion (11.7%) of total retail sales.[14] Online sales have seen a significant growth because of the internet. The progression of the internet and technology will continually add value to business and customer relationships and provide material for future marketing research.

Customers are moving toward the internet to develop

---

[14] https://www.digitalcommerce360.com/2017/02/17/us-e-commerce-sales-grow-156-2016/

knowledge, business insights, and for other personal reasons. Research has shown that businesses that utilize traditional marketing techniques and advertising methods have seen a decrease in revenue because consumers are moving online to search for businesses and make purchases. Considering the exceptional growth of the internet, businesses without a viable marketing strategy embracing the internet witnessed a lack of marketing effectiveness, product sales, and brand awareness. To counter the effects of the interpersonal communication that the internet presents, your business should obviously develop strategic marketing communication for targeting internet-based customers.

Using the internet to gather information aids in collecting pertinent data for better comprehending the perceptions of your customers toward your business. Given the development of the internet, you can utilize technology for storing and accumulating customer information. Likewise, because of the significant influence of the internet, you can also use the internet to help with establishing relationships with business partners and customers.

The internet affects individuals in their daily lives and can produce challenges for your business due to the accessibility of social media. Online networking has revealed an entryway for customers to express their concerns directly to your business, and this method of correspondence encourages interaction between your business and your customers. Subsequently, customers appreciate having their sentiments validated. However, the immediate and open forum of communication could present challenges for your business if you are not prepared to manage and grow with the online trend.

Customers have a significant influence on the brand awareness of your business as the opinions of customers can propel your brand reputation. For instance, inquiries, comments, and reactions on discussion boards often affect brand loyalty, social following, and purchasing habits. Given the internet, you have to carefully monitor your brand, public activities, and reputation if you want to stay ahead of customer concerns and problems that could impact your sales and business growth.

## DISRUPTIVE TECHNOLOGY

Disruptive Technology (DT) is a powerful means of broadening and developing new markets and providing new functionality, which, in turn, may disrupt existing market linkages. DT is when a new technology upsets the way that things have been. An example of DT is the radio replacing the newspaper, or the television replacing the radio as a source of news. DT is not when a single event occurs that disrupts things. It is when a process plays out over time that causes new technology to either replace or reduce the use of an older method.

DT can be beneficial to your business considering it offers more opportunity or options to your customers and influences product innovation. By not adopting DT, your business could potentially miss opportunities for a financial gain and powerful tools that could make your business more productive. A concern with DT is that it often takes away from you or your employee having to think for yourself. An example would be a calculator replacing the deep analysis of problem-solving, or digital navigation systems causing its users to not have to remember directions, or a cell phone contact list that makes it so that you don't have to remember a phone number. With so much dependent upon these technologies that we rely on to help us in our day-to-day, we can become lost without the benefits that DT has created.

DT is not always used as a method to remove or replace traditional methods; it can also create an alternative to the way things are done. It creates typically simpler, more convenient, and less expensive ways of doing things. DT is usually a result of the desire to make things easier, faster, and more convenient. Hence, landline telephones and traditional mail services are now second to cell phones and email.

Not everyone has or will adapt to DT. Just as cell phones have not fully replaced the landline, DT ultimately could have a major impact on an existing market without totally displacing it. Not everyone uses the internet or a mobile device in place of reading a book, looking through a map, or earning a degree. Many individuals still select to drive a car, take a train, or travel by boat to get to their destination.

There are, however, ways in which DT has caused those unwilling to adopt it, to make sacrifices. Video streaming services Redbox and Netflix have caused brick-and-mortar businesses such as Blockbuster to close shop because of Blockbusters inability to create or adapt to DT. Digital photography caused film to become practically obsolete. DT introduces threats to existing methods, but also opportunities for new sources of competitive advantages. The benefits of DT go to the risk takers. Without being willing to take risks, the individual or business would never accept DT. Risk taking, however, can have negative impacts if it is not executed properly and with a strategic plan. For DT to be successful, small businesses and individuals must weigh the benefits. Without proper knowledge and training of why DT is needed or how to use it for success, the transition will likely fail and DT will negatively disrupt your business.

## TRENDS AND INNOVATION

For innovation to be advantageous within your business, you must have a strategy for informing customers on the specific benefits of the trend or innovation in relation to your product or service. Trends affected by customer choices, the internet, social media, and technology have a greater influence on customer behavior than conventional advertising. As a leader, you should develop strategies incorporating a knowledge of trends and areas identifying with technology, internet, innovation, and social media.

**Technology Trends.** Technology influences customers regarding business sustainability and corporate responsibility. Emerging innovative technology can propel your business to growth by providing a medium for evaluating choice patterns of your customers. The advancement of technology can additionally influence the value of your products and services. Moreover, by using technology, you could develop strategies that decidedly enhance your perceived product value. You can additionally utilize innovative technology to improve marketing research knowledge. For technology to remain beneficial within your markets, your business must have a system for effectively using technology to train and educate customers on the benefits of your product or service.

**Technology in Marketing.** Marketing is not shaped by what technology can do but instead centers on what the customer will accept, understand, and want. There are three changes that you must consider when creating successful marketing strategies using technology. The first is to move away from market research and instead look toward being able to interpret information extracted from your customers through databases of information. The second change is to move away from traditional advertising and placing more attention on social media for communication. The final stage is to stop looking at marketing as a means of mass markets and move toward building a personal relationship with customers through media outlets.

## NETWORK COMMUNICATION

Major trends in technology that could impact communication within your business include; voice over internet protocol (VOIP), web 2.0, and virtual networks. Unlike virtual networks, face-to-face (F2F) meetings provide limited support for global projects and establishments. Within virtual networks, a powerful infrastructure and high-speed data services are required from both network users to help prevent interruption of communication, which is likely on slower connections. Technologies used throughout virtual networks include; email, chat, phone, video conference, group calendars, and other electronic meeting systems. F2F meetings can be good to set the stage for a growing relationship. However, technological communication presents an opportunity for the relationship to continually develop.

Trust has been connected to the success of virtual software communication, and F2F communication is often beneficial in helping to establish trust and social ties. Trust is a requirement when working to build social ties and relationships, but difficult to build at a distance. Consequently, virtual teams have a difficult time establishing relationships and are often more prone to conflict. For global projects, individuals should be acquainted with one another prior to joining in virtual communication considering the original meeting builds trust. Considering most organizations have upgraded their structure to utilize technology and information processing systems, allowing local employees to work and communicate virtually can increase your business's productivity by lowering delays in communication.

# SOCIAL MEDIA

The development of the internet has created challenges for businesses who fail to grow with the technology or properly manage social media. Social media has opened a door for customers to express their concerns to or about companies and this method of communication gives customers the power of opinion and change. Customers are a significant factor in generating brand awareness for businesses. This is due to users promoting the brand as well as creating content and exposure through social comments, questions, and answers on forum boards and social media profiles.

Because of technology and social media, the customer has the power to help improve and enrich business activities as well as add value to brands. Considering customers are paramount to the success of your business, your marketing strategies must move away from traditional transactional marketing to facilitator marketing. Facilitator marketing focuses on sharing knowledge with your customers and being open to the opinions of your customers. This method will assist in promoting positive sales and satisfied customers.

## SOCIAL MEDIA MARKETING

Whether you want to call it social media or web 2.0, businesses have started joining into one of the fastest growing industries around. A survey by McKinsey & Company showed that nearly 1,700 businesses using web 2.0 technologies had increased conversions, developed successful marketing strategies, increased communication, and had a greater ability to provide better products. The most often-reported business benefits of web 2.0 were a greater ability to share ideas, improved (and faster) access to knowledge experts, and reduced costs of communication, travel, and operations.

Your social media marketing plan should include creating an online presence within the micro-blogging networks including Facebook and Twitter. By using an online platform such as Twitter and Facebook, your business can promote the brand by blogging updates about the company and interacting with followers and subscribers. Along with blogging, other benefits of using a social media platform are:

- Video updating and posting of ads and commercials
- Sharing photos of events your company may have had or attended
- Discussion – allowing followers to ask questions directly from these platforms
- Link placement – adding backlinks to your main website
- Networking – interacting with current and potential customers

Facebook stats:

- More than 2 billion monthly active users
- 1.74 billion active mobile users
- Five new profiles are created every second
- 4.75 billion pieces of content shared daily
- More than 50 million active small businesses have active Pages on Facebook
- Average user spends more than 20 minutes per day on Facebook

Twitter stats:

- Total audience of roughly 317 million monthly active users.
- Users are averaging 6,000 tweets per second. 500 million per day.
- 80% of users access site via mobile devices.
- 83% of the world's leaders are on Twitter.

Instagram stats:

- 500 million active monthly users.
- 95 million photos and videos shared daily.
- Used by 48.8% of U.S. brands.

- 75% of users take action, such as visiting a website, after looking at an Instagram ad post.

**Mobile Social Marketing.** Along with promoting your company for free, social media platforms allow users to interact with your business from their mobile devices. Facebook, Twitter, and Instagram are some of the most popular services that your business should use to market toward mobile customers. Knowing this will allow your business to further market to these users on their mobile devices, which could help increase and expand your marketing efforts and brand awareness for little or no cost.

Social media networks make it simple for customers to follow or become fans of your business. These platforms are relatively easy for customers to sign up and start receiving updates from your business. You can also use these platforms to provide customers with article updates, blogs, discounts, and portfolio updates.

Customers can use social media to interact with your business by contributing to status updates, articles, blogs, and other news and images posted by your company. Marketing on these social platforms gives your business the opportunity to post information on corporate accomplishments and share links to your website, promotional sites, and other press release pages.

Social media benefits include:

- The ability to offer 'insider' discounts, specials, and other values to followers only.
- Participating in online social media groups will allow for building a more personal relationship with past and potential customers.
- Allows for quick access for customers to ask questions.

By building your website using a CMS, you can easily integrate it with your social media accounts. You should also add a plug-in to your website linked to your social profiles using an Application Programming Interface (API), often provided by the social media networks. Facebook, Twitter, and other popular social media networks also have API plugins that help link the networks together with other social media platforms and websites, so that if information on one platform is updated, it will also update the other networks automatically. Metrics used in Google Analytics can help show which platform users link from, how they explore your website, and how visitor experiences can be enhanced. With this information, you can improve your ROI, increase conversions, and ultimately make more money on the web.

**Customer Tracking.** Tracking customers allow you to see how effective, or ineffective, your social marketing strategies are and which customers and customer segments are most responsive to your strategies. Tracking also helps to see what users like and dislike by analyzing bounce rate and the amount of time customers spend on your website, and which pages resonate with prospects and lead to conversions. Using this metrics system, you get a better understanding of the site content customers are most interested in and find out how effective your current content is.

# VIRAL MARKETING

Social media marketing (SMM) is a form of internet marketing which is used to help achieve branding and marketing communication goals through participation on social media. SMM is a great way to better market your business online. Having a social networking presence for your business and interacting with potential customers is a great way to expand your brand name and awareness.

The benefit of a viral SMM plan is the ability to create a video that focuses on entertaining the customer while providing valuable information about your brand and what it offers. The video should provide information on the benefits of the business. The concept of the video should be informative and is intended to encourage viewers to share the video via social media and on websites where they are a member. After watching the video, the customer should be inspired to visit your company, call, visit your website, and share the viral marketing video and the information about your company to their friends. A viral marketing plan should be distributed via video and social networking sites such as YouTube, Twitter, Facebook, and by using other multimedia embedding networks and websites. A viral marketing plan can easily create a positive image for your brand while also providing valuable promotional content to users.

# CHAPTER 9

# The Price of Communication

## REPUTATION MANAGEMENT

Customer feedback and reviews are influential and can affect how your customers engage with your businesses. The influence of a review is dependent on the value the reader of the review places on the individual who posted the review. Additionally, potential customers use reviews to pre-qualify your business by gaining insight into the ethics, products, and services your business offers. For reviews to be influential, the review must be honest, credible, and written by actual customers and not your business's marketing department. However, the effect of influencer marketing is decreasing as customers have come to realize that businesses can influence the selection of reviews as a marketing tactic.

Your business should utilize product reviews as a means to improve sales and validate successful experiences and problem areas with current and potential customers. When developing marketing strategies, you should make an effort to take note of reviewer demographics and characteristics. A survey by comScore, an internet marketing and advertising company, found that 24% of online customers thoughtfully considered online reviews prior to making a purchase.[15] By examining the influence of reviews and eventual product sales in relation to commonalities between products and customers, marketing managers seeking to gain insight into the shopping and purchasing behaviors of customers can use these reviews as a method of obtaining information.

The value of customer reviews depends on the quality of the review and its substance, the credibility of the reviewer, and the nature of the review in addition to the number of reviews in total, the average review score, and the overall consensus of the reviewers. The internet provides numerous venues for customers and marketing managers to share and receive product knowledge through the sharing of experiences and insights. Customer-generated reviews were considered more trustworthy and credible than any other form of correspondence. Moreover, using the internet permitted customers to purchase products effortlessly and conveniently through websites including Amazon.com and eBay.com which permitted customers to search and compare products, brands, and reviews. In addition to the value of products, customers consider reviews, seller notoriety, and promotional product photos to be the most influential elements that contribute to making final purchasing decisions.

Some of your customers will be fundamentally influenced by information posted by previous customers and will consider those reviews most credible and trustworthy. Content style,

---

[15] Ritchie, J., Lewis, J., Nicholls, C. M., & Ormston, R. (Eds.). (2013). Qualitative research practice: A guide for social science students and researchers (2nd ed.). Los Angeles, CA: Sage Publications.

source, and peripheral credibility cues in social reviews influence customer beliefs. It's often difficult to discern the credibility of customer reviews, and your customers' perception of reviews is a distinguishing factor in purchasing intentions. Therefore, expert reviews provide more credibility and trustworthiness, while guest reviewers, new reviewers, and reviewers with a low number of posts tend to lack credibility.

Online customer reviews constitute a focal point for evaluating customer decision making in terms of online purchases. The quality of customer reviews has a significant effect on the credibility, trustworthiness, and as a result, the perception of your business. Customers use reviews to help determine the trustworthiness of your business based on the ratings and quality of reviews. In using a web-based experiment to examine the quality and effect of product reviews on study participants' decisions, research found that customers rated reviews based on the quality and the extent of the reviews. High-quality reviews were adequately detailed and generated positive evaluations. In a study of 577 participants, researchers concluded that expert opinions had a significant influence on the perception of reviews, as did visual presentations of reviews. Furthermore, observable characteristics of products had a notable effect on product perception and reviews.[16]

Reviews encourage purchases by helping to avoid confusion and limiting choice overload. Customer reviews and word-of-mouth have always played significant roles in marketing campaigns in that they help to increase product sales, reduce price sensitivity, and increase customer knowledge which helps to reduce the uncertainty of purchasing and increases customer satisfaction. After testing a sample of 203 customer review

---

[16] Situmeang, F. B., Leenders, M. A., & Wijnberg, N. M. (2014). History matters: The impact of reviews and sales of earlier versions of a product on consumer and expert reviews of new editions. European Management Journal, 32, 73-83. doi:10.1016/j.emj.2013.11.001

community participants on OpenRice.com, researchers determined that 69% of the participants shared reviews and rated the quality of those reviews based on various factors including reputation, sense of belonging, and the joy of helping others.[17]

## IMPACT OF REVIEWS ON MARKETING OBJECTIVE

Customer engagement is critical when working to develop brand awareness and increase sales. Negative customer reviews affect small businesses significantly more than larger businesses. Consequently, depending upon your business size, customer reviews may not always have a significant influence on your profitability. Additionally, reviews, whether positive or negative, do not have a significant influence on customers familiar with your business. Similar to a tree in the forest, a review alone is not going to gain or lose new business for a client, but can help to sway a potential customer to make a decision either way. Engaging with customers is a strategy recommended by marketing agencies to create a competitive advantage by building relationships with customers. If the objective of your business is customer acquisition, retention, or brand awareness, then customer reviews can affect your marketing strategy development.

Because of social media, customer feedback and reviews can quickly reach a broad audience and have an immediate effect on the success of your business's marketing efforts. Due to the popularity of the internet, you can analyze and predict customer behaviors by using social networks and review-based websites. Your business should spend marketing dollars wisely, so gaining more reviews is not always as important as generating brand awareness through other reliable methods of marketing. Your

[17] Cheung, C. M., & Lee, M. K. (2012). What drives consumers to spread electronic word of mouth in online consumer-opinion platforms. Decision Support Systems, 53, 218-225. doi:10.1016/j.dss.2012.01.015

marketing strategies should focus on relationship building with customers to better develop successful strategies for increasing customer loyalty and sales. However, you are likely not effectively accomplishing your marketing objective if you are receiving a significant amount of negative reviews.

## ELECTRONIC WORD-OF-MOUTH

Customers often use social media channels when purchasing products or services. Social media channels including Facebook, Amazon, and Yelp are greater influences than electronic word-of-mouth communication on business websites and testimonials. Electronic word-of-mouth (eWOM) has a significant influence on the success of your business, and has become a major factor in customer decision-making processes.

The main contrast between traditional word-of-mouth and eWOM is that eWOM has a greater reach and accelerated interaction. Considering the simplicity of accessing eWOM reviews, your business should progressively seek to analyze related factors and outcomes influencing eWOM. Electronic word-of-mouth goes far beyond traditional word-of-mouth to include online communication and networking through social forums, review sites, and news sites. Therefore, your sales are highly dependent on eWOM influences. Moreover, eWOM affects the trust and perception of your business, and the products you offer. When there is a large number of positive eWOM referrals, sales and business profits are likely to increase.

## SOCIAL MEDIA REVIEWS

Online networking is a gathering of internet-based applications built on the foundation of ideology and technical specifications of web 2.0, which allows for the development and exchange of user-generated content. Social media is a critical area of enthusiasm for marketing managers and practitioners seeking to evaluate and influence customers' perceptions. Researchers found that 88% of marketers used social media and spent over $60 billion per year consistently on social media marketing. The most valuable social media tools for gathering marketing data are LinkedIn®, Twitter, Facebook, and online blogging. [18] The essential marketing applications of social media include content marketing, market research, and business networking.

Your business should use social media for presenting marketing endeavors and building relationships with customers. Having an influential social presence is critical to propelling your marketing and brand development strategies. Increasing knowledge, implementing social media strategies, and brand showcasing can benefit your business by exploiting the opportunities that social networks present. In conducting a study consisting of 236 social media users' online interactions to evaluate predictors relating to social media sites, it was found that online networking had a significant effect on customers' perceptions of online marketing and advertisements.[19]

In a large-scale field experiment comprising of 45,000 participants of an online mall, researchers found that both financial and value incentives were significant forces in generating brand awareness through social members.[20] If you grasp how to capitalize from online discussions, you can develop strategies that enhance your business's reputation, profits, and brand awareness. Social influence is characterized as a propensity to accept data as evidence about reality. For instance, with online movie ratings, customers frequently rate movies based on previous ratings by

[18] Whiting, A., & Williams, D. (2013). Why people use social media: A uses and gratifications approach. Qualitative Market Research: An International Journal, 16, 362-369. doi:10.1108/qmr-06-2013-0041
[19] Vinerean, S., Cetina, I., Dumitrescu, L., & Tichindelean, M. (2013). The effects of social media marketing on online consumer behavior. International Journal of Business and Management, 8, 66. doi:10.5539/ijbm.v8n14p66
[20] Ahrens, J., Coyle, J. R., & Strahilevitz, M. A. (2013). Electronic word of mouth: The effects of incentives on e-referrals by senders and receivers. European Journal of Marketing, 47, 1034-1051. doi:10.1108/03090561311324192

other customers. This happens because customers using social media have a significant influence on the actions and suppositions of their peer groups.

The advantage of using social media for your business is to connect with those customers who can decidedly influence your brand's notoriety and awareness. For an individual to be influential on social media, they need to present relevant substance within their reviews and have a reasonable social following. You could gain influential power by identifying, reaching, and bargaining with customers online. To develop these relationships of power, you should solicit influential customers and provide product samples and ask that they share their evaluations and feedback on social networks.

## MONITORING REVIEWS

Monitoring social networks for customer reviews enables your business to develop customer relationships, which can enhance your business's reputation and value. Customer reviews require an immediate need to respond, particularly when working toward preventing negative reviews from influencing potential customers.

To monitor and identify customer reviews, the use of a review monitoring tool that enables you to acknowledge positive reviewers and perform conflict resolution for negative reviews is a worthwhile expenditure. When a customer posts a review, that review has the potential to spread to a larger audience. There are services including Bazaar Voice and Yelp that help with monitoring customer reviews. You should use these review monitoring tools for proactive crisis management and conflict resolution for negative reviews, and to acknowledge and share positive reviews.

# REPUTATION MANAGEMENT

Reputation management is an essential aspect of marketing, and the posted opinions of your customers on social media, and how your business connects with those customers, aids in generating brand awareness and marketing success. You cannot control customer reviews. Consequently, it is imperative that you continually monitor and manage social networks. To help maintain the reputation of your business, an automated system can be used to e-mail noted positive reviewers and request that they post reviews on multiple social media networks to increase the exposure of these positive reviews. You should also consider offering special status, VIP sales, unique merchandising promos, or other perks to these select individuals to retain their interest in championing your business within their social sphere.

In response to determining the management of customer reviews, you should not ignore the opinions of customers. Reviews are free pathways for gaining insights into customers' perspectives compared to incentives, surveys, and focus groups. Unlike positive reviews, negative reviews have a greater likelihood of generating negative emotions and business perceptions. Reputation managers should have crisis management training for comprehending the proper steps for knowing how to de-escalate emotional situations that drive to the heart of the customer's issues without the manager being emotionally invested. No matter the ranking or quality of the review, you should listen to the concerns of the reviewer, address the issues, and prevent customer dissatisfaction from happening in the future. When customers write reviews, particularly negative reviews, they expect a response from your business. Acknowledging customer reviews could benefit your marketing strategy by gaining insights into unforeseen problems within your business.

# REVIEW CREDIBILITY

Knowing the platforms on which customers prefer to express their views, and on which readers of those reviews are most likely to visit, is essential for effective online management.

**Review Websites.** Review platforms including Yelp, Amazon, Angie's List, TripAdvisor, and more heavily influence consumers when researching desired products and services. Unfortunately, these sites, and others, often end up authorizing unauthenticated reviews and manipulated reviews on their websites which could unduly damage the reputation of your business. For instance, the Yelp platform contains an algorithm that automatically determines which reviews are "most useful" without actually authenticating the reviews. This is because, like many other review sites, Yelp has no verification process in place to validate whether the reviewer actually participated in any transaction with the business in question, which enables fraudulent reviews by Yelp users and business competitors. After analyzing the writing style of reviewers and the effectiveness of manipulated reviews through sentiments, readability, and ratings, researchers have determined that 10.3% of products were subject to online review manipulation.[21]

## NEGATIVE REVIEWS

Review credibility is important, particularly in situations where reviews falsely or purposefully misrepresent a situation. Your business should develop an appropriate response to counter the effects of negative word-of-mouth (NWOM) communication. How your business responds to NWOM is crucial in terms of limiting the negative effects to the business.

Sensory marketing helps to identify and comprehend the

---

[21] Fan, Y. W., Miao, Y. F., Fang, Y. H., & Lin, R. Y. (2013). Establishing the adoption of electronic word-of-mouth through consumers' perceived credibility. International Business Research, 6. doi:10.5539/ibr.v6n3p58

senses and influences of marketing engagement in light of customers' perceptions, behaviors, and judgments. How your business reacts to NWOM is critical in determining whether your business can recuperate from the negative reviews and feedback. While positive reviews do have an influence on customer decision making, one negative review from a disgruntled customer generally has a more significant effect on overall product ratings. Conversely, negative reviews have less of an influence when contrasted to a vast majority of positive reviews.

While you may be aware of the effects of customer reviews, do not succumb to the temptation of generating fake reviews to help promote your products or services. The drawback of manipulated reviews is that they could unduly damage the reputation of your business. Respond to customer reviews in a timely and effective manner as they influence customers' perceptions of your business. Your business should place a priority on responding to both positive and negative reviews. Don't ignore negative feedback, as from an overall brand perspective, negative reviews have the potential to hinder brand awareness by creating customer doubt which can decrease leads and referrals.

## REVIEW RESPONSE

With the popularity of social media and the internet, customers have come to expect businesses to engage and respond quickly to questions and complaints. A primary marketing objective is to always to leave customers with a positive feeling about your business and the services provided. It is necessary to know how to engage with customers to influence positive feedback and relationships. Developing effective correspondence is the first step in accomplishing brand loyalty and supports the development of positive relationships with customers. An internal and external support staff tasked with monitoring your website, social media sites, twitter, and the like is beneficial in helping you to identify customer reviews, especially negative reviews, and in helping you work through any conflicts by addressing the reviewer and resolving their concerns.

When responding to customer reviews, the objective is to make certain the message is positive, the matter is resolved, and the customer is satisfied with the outcome. Considering most customer reviews are on social media networks, the individual responsible for responding to customer reviews should have cognitive writing skills and a good compass for creating appropriate responses. Researchers found that 72% of customers wrote negative reviews with the expectation that businesses would respond and take responsibility.[22] Empathy, compassion, and having the ability to relate are the primary characteristics needed of an effective review responder. Responses should be prepared in advance to prevent your business from scrambling for a response at the last minute.

How to respond to a review is dependent on the type of review received. If the response is negative, in addition to replying, you should communicate with the reviewer via phone or e-mail to quickly resolve the issue. The best course of action is to respond tactfully, and in a timely manner, and then work with the customer to prevent future problems or concerns from occurring. When a customer writes a review, you should respond promptly with a quality resolution to the customer's concern. Furthermore, you should respond promptly to negative reviews to prevent customers from posting the review elsewhere and sharing it with other customers. In addition to empathy, compassion, and problem solving you should have the ability to investigate and satisfy the customer's issues.

---

[22] Gurău, C. (2012). Solving customer complaints: A study of multiple commercial settings. Annals of the University of Oradea, Economic Science Series, 21, 827-833. Retrieved from http://anale.steconomiceuoradea.ro

# COMPLAINT REPAIRING STRATEGY

When responding to a customer complaint, your business should have one main goal, to defend your brand. The first step in the process is to check the information to figure out who wrote the complaint and why they wrote it. This information can likely be found by analyzing the complaint to find hints of information about the author. Normally, those who leave complaints don't leave their true identity or contact information. Once you find who wrote the complaint, you should put together a response. The complaint response should be well written, should answer the complainant somewhat directly, and should come directly from a respected position within the business with high authority.

The department that worked with the customer should write the response, and it should be edited and signed by the company's CEO. This will allow for a filtering of the response that will rid it of any emotional attachments. In addition to putting together a response, your company should also check the damage of the complaint. You may also want to check other complaint boards for additional reviews and the search engine rank of the complaint to see how much damage it has or can do to your reputation. If the complaint has initiated a series of additional complaints, your company should look to respond promptly to the complaint. To assess the true spread of the complaint, you can use search engines such as Google, Yahoo, and Bing. With these search engines, you can search the name of your business and see which complaints show up and respond to them from highest to lowest rankings. The goal of the response is for your business to confront the mistake and seek a resolution.

In addition, your company should project a positive image of the business and include alternative methods for complainants to report any issues in the future. This alternative method should include either the website's testimonial or rating section, using the contact form on the company website, or information for contacting the company CEO. The goal of providing links and email addresses to these in-house sources is to prevent future complaints on third-party websites. The most reliable solution to a complaint is gained through direct contact with the complainant to solve the issue at hand. Once they are satisfied with the results, you should ask the customer if they would be polite enough to remove, edit, or request removal of the complaint. Simply listening to the customer's concern and coming to a mutual understanding can easily resolve most complaints.

## CRISIS MANAGEMENT

Case in point: After the launch of the Fitbit Force, a wrist-worn product that tracks fitness activity, 1.7% of more than 100 million users began developing skin rashes where the device was being worn. CEO James Park, responded almost immediately to the news, delivering an apology and initiating a product recall with a full refund for all of the devices. Later, test results showed that users were likely experiencing allergic contact dermatitis which is an itchy rash and caused largely by a substance that comes into contact with the skin. The likely cause of the rash, in these instances, was users not properly cleansing the area of their skin beneath the device, which was very often worn all day, every day. The Fitbit Company could have easily blamed the rash on user error, but instead decided to take full responsibility and issue a recall. Instead of dealing with customer backlash, due to the company's timely, and proactive response, the company continues to do well, having maintained their integrity in the marketplace as well as the trust of their customer base.

At the other end of the spectrum, Kryptonite, a leading manufacturer of bicycle locks, had a crisis in 2004. After an internet video had surfaced of a user hacking the well-respected company's lock, many more videos and complaints began forming. The videos showed how the lock could be easily unlocked by jamming it with a plastic pen. Kryptonite eventually did address the situation, but weeks later, with a product recall and an explanation that the issue dealt with all types of cylinder locks including those associated with vending machines and some automobile ignitions. Because it took the company an extended period of time to respond, customers and the media continued to smear the company's brand for days. This led to a loss of customer trust and a near irreparably tainted brand. Beyond the cost of the recall, millions of dollars have been spent to rebuild the company's reputation.

When dealing with a crisis, the focus is centered on brand trust and risk. A crisis should be addressed through direct contact whenever possible as in the case of Fitbit where users received an email from the CEO about the recall versus the use of mass social media. It is also important to recognize that media outlets and third parties have the capability to either preserve or damage customer-to-brand trust. Consumer relationships and widespread brand trust are essential during a crisis, and your business cannot afford to neglect the element of the media if you want to retain customers. Marketing strategies during a crisis should also project that your company remains adaptive and is present during the crisis.

# CHAPTER 10

## Do The Right Thing

## PRIVACY AND ETHICS

### EMAIL SPAMMING

Studies are conducted on websites to discover how often current and potential customers visit, and make return visits, to websites. Often, those numbers are much lower than expected. One solution to gaining more return visits includes bulk email marketing. A Direct Marketing Association study found that email marketing is second only to search engine marketing (SEM) as a top method of driving traffic to websites.[23] Your email marketing tactics should target only users who have specifically

---

[23] "DMA Releases 2010 Response Rate Trend Report," Direct Marketing Association, www.the-dma.org, June 15, 2010.

opted-in to your mailing list to receive updates on new sales, discounts, and other company information. In addition, these campaigns can drastically lower the cost of developing promotional direct mailings including savings on printing, packaging, and postage. Email marketing is also known to yield a much higher response rate than traditional mailings.

**Email SPAM.** If you have ever heard of the term bulk marketing, then you have probably also heard the term SPAM used to describe it. SPAM is the acronym used for Specifically Persecuted Advertising Mail. The term spam was first introduced in the early 1990s to describe e-mail messages not related to the topic of discussion and postings that swamped newsgroups. SPAM is frequently described as e-mail that is sent in bulk; flooding the internet with copies of the same message and forcing these unwanted messages on to users who might otherwise have chosen not to receive them. Most SPAM is commercial advertising and has received the negative title of SPAM due to its subject matter often relating to dubious products, get-rich-quick schemes, or quasi-legal services.

**The CAN-SPAM Act.** The CAN-SPAM Act was introduced in 2003 and is an acronym which stands for, Controlling the Assault of Non-Solicited Pornography and Marketing. This law was the United States' first attempt at a national regulation with regard to the sending of commercial email. In addition, it gives email recipients the right to opt-out of receiving unwanted messages. The CAN-SPAM Act includes tough penalties for those who are caught spamming without abiding by the rule of law. Violation of the CAN-SPAM Act is subject to penalties of up to $16,000.

A well-known case involving spam concerned the popular social networking site Facebook, Sanford Wallace, and two others. In February 2009, it was alleged that Sanford used phishing sites or other means to fraudulently gain access to Facebook accounts and used them to distribute phishing SPAM throughout the network. The result of this case was that Sanford was charged and was made to pay a fine of $711 million dollars. This is an example of an extreme case of spamming that had a perfectly reasonable outcome. The reality is that unsolicited SPAM has absolutely no benefits. It is unethical, has notoriously low conversion rates, and can land you in jail — or leave you owing millions of dollars in fines.

While spamming is illegal, bulk email marketing is perfectly legal. The difference is that bulk email marketing campaigns consist of an opted-in list of users who have signed up to join a mailing list because they were interested in your product or service. If you do send bulk email, be aware that, despite its name, the CAN-SPAM Act does not only apply to bulk email. It covers all commercial messages, which the law defines as any electronic mail message that has a primary purpose of commercial advertisement or promotion of a commercial product or service. This also includes emails that promote a commercial website and its content. The rules cover messages that are sent to current or previous customers, and include exceptions for business-to-business emails.

Your goal should be to create an easily accessible and convenient way for your website visitors to opt-in to receive promotional emails and newsletters. Market your email program as you would any other effort to encourage customer engagement. Obtain their contact information in the form of their email address in addition to their mailing address, and let the customer state their preferred method of interaction. However, it is important, in terms of a marketing strategy, to entice them to utilize email to receive timely notifications of current sales, discounts, and promotions. Remember, while the First Amendment gives you the freedom to say what it is that you want to say, it works best when you say it to people who want to hear it.

- **Guidelines for legal email communications**: Don't use false or misleading header information. Clearly state what the email is about and what users can expect. Match your headings to the message body. If the body of the message is to promote your upcoming sale, your header should read: "Save on …." Don't use deceptive subject lines. If you are looking to promote a 10% discount on your customized product for a particular month: the subject title should read, "Save 10% on customizing…." If the message is an advertisement, it should be clearly identified as one.

- Emails must contain the company's address and other contact information.

- Provide users with a way to opt-out of receiving any further mailings.

## ETHICS

Research has found that 75% of employees do not desire to work for businesses with poor organizational ethics.[24] Beginning in 2003, many businesses created a new staff position titled Ethics Officer to satisfy work ethics, increase awareness of positive ethics in business, and safeguard the company's position in the marketplace. Ethical considerations within businesses are largely overlooked, and most business ethics research is susceptible to interaction biases.

**Organizational Ethics.** Organizational ethics is the study

---

[24] Chekwa, C., Ouhirra, L., Thomas, E., & Chukwuanu, M. (2014). An examination of the effects of leadership on business ethics: Empirical study. International Journal Of Business & Public Administration, 11(1), 48-65.

and evaluation of decision-making processes by business leaders according to moral concepts and judgments. An ethical theory is a system that provides rules that guide individuals in making decisions. Organizational ethics are determined by the standards, principles, and moral intentions by which a business operates. **Ethical behavior** provides a foundation for understanding what constitutes a moral human being. **Unethical behavior** is regarded as an act which violates accepted moral norms of behavior.

Make certain that your business has implemented codes of ethics and that your employees are aware of these policies. It is your responsibility as a business leader to inform and educate your employees about your policies, considering that you will be held accountable when ethics are not satisfied. Many business professionals believe that ethics are unimportant in the field of business. They further believe that the only obligation they have to their business is to maximize profits. By not implementing and satisfying organizational ethics, it could cost your business financial loss, risk your positive reputation, and increase external pressures.

**Ethical Dilemma.** In a multi-part federal investigation of an American Express subsidiary in Utah, American Express was found to have violated customer protection laws from every stage of the customer experience from marketing to debt collecting. Several American Express companies were found to have violated protection laws provided for customers. The illegal activities were discovered during a routine examination of an American Express subsidiary by The Federal Deposit Corporation and the Utah Department of Financial Institutions. American Express was found to have violated federal law in billing, debt collection practices, and marketing. In the same year, the Customer Financial Protection Bureau enforced actions against Capital One and Discover Financial over sales tactics.

So, what happened? American Express, along with Discover and Capital One failed to monitor their third-party vendors. The activity had occurred at the American Express Centurion Bank, the American Express Travel Related Services Company, Inc., and American Express Bank, FSB. The violations included deception, unlawful late fee charges, age discrimination, failure to report customer disputes to reporting agencies, and misleading customers about debt collection. In 2012, American Express was required to refund $85 million dollars to customers for illegal card practices that took place between 2002 and spring 2012. Though the act was unethical, American Express leaders fully cooperated with authorities and began their own investigation into the matter. They eventually found and reported additional fraud and violations. American Express agreed to end the illegal practices of their subsidiaries, fully refund approximately 250,000 customers who were affected, implement new compliance procedures, and pay a civil monetary penalty of $27.5 million. Court orders also required American Express to change their business practices so that a similar situation would be avoided in the future.

As the Chief Executive Officer of American Express since 2001, Kenneth Chenault stated in an interview that, no matter how strong or ethical a company is they are going to experience some difficulty. He further noted that leadership was paramount during these difficult times. Chenault stated that if leaders could not be ethical in times of crisis, they would lose credibility and followership. As a leader, ethics determine what is done in decision-making situations. Ethical leaders are concerned about justice, fairness, and treating subordinates equally. Additionally, leaders with an ethical identity are likely to affect the self-concepts, beliefs, and attitudes of their followers.

Chenault's belief is that if leaders are not focused on moral ethics and integrity, they will not be successful. He further explained that to create ethics within an organization, it begins with leadership. The best-run companies are those that encourage employees to raise issues based on their ethics.

When responding to an unethical situation of its subsidiaries, American Express acted ethically by cooperating and coming forward with valuable information that could help the investigation, and ensure that the customer would be fully refunded. American Express corrected the matter by putting together plans to correct each of the violations and worked to strengthen its internal compliance processes. By correcting the matter and admitting to its faults, American Express may have maintained their brand reliability and business's ethical standards. Had the situation not been resolved, American Express may have tarnished their brand's reputation, trust, status, and lost customers because of their unethical tactics.

Businesses are often focused on the pursuit of self-interest, and it is human nature not to ask questions about why things are going well. Situations such as the one with American Express place pressure on organizations and their leaders to behave ethically at all times. It was the responsibility of American Express to hold their subsidiaries accountable for their lack of ethics. To resolve unethical situations in your business, you should implement ethical standards that align with your industry, the law, and your personal beliefs. Additionally, ethics officers can assist your business in developing codes of ethics and enforcing ethical codes as needed.

## PRIVACY

There is a growing concern from customers that their privacy and personal information is being digitized and sold without their permission. The concern is that credit cards, billing details, and other private data are bought and sold across the marketing industry between businesses and organizations to use as soliciting tools. Customers agree that the lack of organizational ethics when collecting information is morally wrong. The debate amongst customers and businesses is that both parties feel they own the information. Businesses believe that they have the right to use the information any way they choose to help better their organizational goals and to produce better marketing services. Additionally, the organizations that purchase the user information feel they own the data because they purchased it. If the results show that your company is being unethical by confusing or misinforming customers on how their private information is used, you should work diligently to resolve the confusion by making privacy details clear.

**Security Breach and Ethics.** You should focus on making ethical decisions when handling customer information in regards to implementing effective security and privacy measures. Many organizations, including healthcare corporations, spend thousands to millions of dollars on securing patient privacy and protecting data against breaches and hackers. It is your responsibility as a leader to understand and influence ethical practices which relate to privacy and security threats. Security breaches can disable the functions of your business and pilfer confidential customer information such as personal contact information, social security numbers, and passwords. In addition to a potential loss of revenue, breaches also create customer distrust, and can negatively impact your brand reputation. The risks associated with breaches such as loss of confidentiality, integrity, and availability should cause you to be aware and proactive with threats that generate concerns.

## TRANSPARENCY IN ORGANIZATIONS

Transparency is defined as the availability of group specific information to those outside of the group. Organizational transparency is when your business information is produced, gathered, validated, or disseminated to outside participants. Transparency can allow for your business to get accelerated feedback on products and services. Being transparent, and informing customers and partners of important business aspects, is seen as an ethical approach to business. For a leader, being transparent creates trust, honesty, accountability, and responsibility. Morally, transparency is important considering that it can affect personal integrity, attitude, and organizational commitment.

An example of a transparent organization is the travel agent industry which moved from traditional travel agencies to online digital offerings. As an online organization, prices, reservations, itineraries, suppliers, and competitive disadvantages became transparent and disrupted traditional sales and brick-and-mortar travel business interests. With current technology and the internet, business transparency is crucial, as is the need to understand the power transparency gives loyal followers. Complete transparency, however, has its setbacks. Your business could lose freedom, secrets, and privacy because of this. Being transparent could also conflict with your moral principles. If your business is transparent, customers can gain knowledge and shared information about available products. Digital transparency also affects competition as competitors can view, compare, and match your prices and products to their advantage. Additionally, full transparency may distract customers and stakeholders from focusing on more important items and information.

## RISK MITIGATION

Organizations have almost become completely dependent on technology to run their everyday operations. In situations where security threats are possible, it is your responsibility as a leader and decision maker to minimize damages and losses generated by security incidents. A major concern with security breaches is that many businesses do not know how to manage or countermeasure the effects. Hackers and phishers are responsible for most online thefts and fraud. These individuals use their abundance of computer knowledge to remotely invade computer systems to access, download, sell, and defraud individuals.

Using, copying, and distributing intellectual software without permission is considered pirating. Forging someone's identity with the intent to use it for fraud is considered identity theft. Your business should have a clear understanding of potential theft vulnerabilities, and have a plan in place to serve as a countermeasure if a breach were ever to occur. You should focus on protecting the major three components of information technology (IT) systems, which include people, information, and IT. Without the proper knowledge, hardware, and data security encryption techniques, you allow your business to be vulnerable to IT security breaches.

A risk management system can be used to monitor and analyze security threats and create countermeasures. Security breaches can disable business functions and pilfer confidential data. No matter the size of your business, you must understand the financial cost of a potential security breach to your company, and protect your business, and your customers from theft and fraud.

# CHAPTER 11

## Working Smarter, Not Harder

## PRODUCTIVITY

The productivity of both you and your business are important. The ethics of your business has a tremendous effect on the morale of the employees. If morale is down, work productivity may also slack. As a leader, you are responsible for creating a healthy environment by supporting your employees. How you lead is crucial in developing productive employees and influencing employee morale and satisfaction. To implement and maintain morale, you should place importance on stress prevention programs and develop effective communication methods with employees to discover and address issues regarding dissatisfaction and potential ethical dilemmas.

## DON'T DO TOO MUCH

One of the biggest business mistakes I have ever made was trying to do everything myself. I wore the hats of the marketing department, sales, customer service, collections, technical support, developer, graphic artist, etc. I understand that you may want to save money or may simply not have the financial support to hire someone to complete additional tasks, however, do what you need to do until you can get help, but get help quickly. If you must take a cut in pay temporarily to hire a project manager while you handle sales, you will be grateful in the end. Otherwise, you will drain yourself dry and never have the time to do what you love. Do yourself a favor and focus on what made you love the idea of being a business owner in the first place.

## MANAGING STRESS

Stress is a negative state often generated by a lack of productivity which can be triggered in the work place by factors including being overworked, disruptive technology, a lack of communication, and a competitive environment. Stress can affect you and your employees' ability to work efficiently. Work overload, uncertainty of future employment, punishment, lack of feedback, and powerlessness are additional causes of stress and can lead to imbalances between you and your employees. Stressful business situations have a tremendous negative impact on employees and productivity, particularly, in situations that involve meeting quotas. Stress can cause you to cut corners and become prone to accidents, abuse, and deception. Several studies have connected stress to memory loss due to an increase in cortisol production. Moreover, employees often respond to stress in a negative manner increasing the likelihood of illness and sick days, poor decision making, and lower rates of production. Data from a study conducted in 2003 by the European Foundation for the Improvement of Living and Working Conditions entitled "Working Conditions in the Acceding and Candidate Countries (Report)" explained that stress was the second largest health problem within business environments, with 22% of organizational members reporting having been affected by stress.

**The main causes of business stress are:**

- Unstable conditions for work activity, which can cause job insecurity.
- Dissatisfaction - common in crisis situations where job restructuring results in a higher level of stress.
- Work hassle - dealing with situations that damage self-esteem and depression.
- Imbalance of time - caused by work overload, which affects the time for personal desires and needs.

**Employee Stress.** In addition to emotional stress, stress can generate high costs for your business in terms of financial loss when factoring in absenteeism, decreased productivity, accidents, legal cost, medical expenses, and staff replacement.

You can assess stress in your business by implementing stress management programs which teach employees techniques to prevent and cope with stressful situations. Stress can be minimized by providing your employees with roles that are clearly defined and encouraging communication between your managers, employees, and other departments. Manager and employee meetings can also be implemented to discuss employee expectations, roles, and concerns. By promoting motivational strategies that positively influence self-esteem, security, and personal achievement, employees would feel valued and less stressed in the work environment.

Stress may be a normal part of your job, and in that case, you have to be able to adjust easily by simply taking a time-out. By putting the stressful task aside and doing some mental problem-solving, you may find a solution to a problem, relieve stress, and may find that the task isn't as stressful when you return to it after having gained a fresh perspective. A break could be a walk outside to get fresh air, a nap, or simply getting away from your desk. The goal is to remove stress by occupying your time and doing something other than the stressful task. You can use similar techniques when dealing with stressful clients, outsourced workers, and business relationships.

The success of your business depends on effectively eliminating occupational stresses that can create frustration, low motivation, personal conflicts, dissatisfaction, and a decrease in productivity. As the leader, you are responsible for reducing the effects of stress and creating an organization that is efficient and stress-free, and one that focuses on maintaining and building the organizations performance. To properly control the climate of your organization, you should try to seek relationships with employees to better understand their personal stressors and work capabilities.

## EMPLOYEE MOTIVATION

Your employees are motivated by many factors including family, finances, and personal well-being. And you have an influence on those motivational factors. In the workplace, employee motivation starts with your leadership or the leadership of their manager. The manager must understand that the employee's family and their personal and financial well-being are key motivational factors in terms of their future within the organization. Having a leader that threatens these motivations will result in the employee putting forth less effort to satisfy their work responsibilities. Moreover, dissatisfied employees would look for ways to leave the company and instead align themselves with a company that positively influences their personal goals and motivations.

## SOURCING WORKLOAD

When it comes to lowering stress levels and accomplishing tasks within your business, there is the option to insource, selfsource, or outsource specific duties. **Insourcing** means to use capable individuals within your business to complete appropriate tasks. **Selfsourcing** is developing and utilizing internal IT systems that can be used by trained workers to complete a wider range of duties. **Outsourcing** is when you choose to use third-party companies or outside individuals to complete tasks.

Outsourcing is growing at an exceptional rate and businesses use outsourcing services provided by individuals throughout the globe. Outsourcing may be an effective solution that can save time and money by providing resources and capabilities outside of the business's structure. In addition, outsourcing allows your business to potentially acquire leading-edge technology without purchasing needed software, updating your current systems, or training employees. Outsourcing allows you to focus your resources on the tasks that matter most and are indicative of your core competencies. Other benefits of outsourcing include lowering development costs, hiring the best talent for the job, and realizing a higher quality of work.

**Short cycle time systems** development involves utilizing methods including automation, outsourcing, and technology to complete tasks quickly. A benefit of this type of structure is that new products and innovation are brought to the marketplace sooner and benefits your business by having a competitive advantage. Concerns with outsourcing short cycle time systems include privacy, security, and potential loss of in-house resources.

The quick reaction of cycle time systems allow the development of new products and services to align with market and environment changes. A disadvantage of producing products or services quickly is that quality may suffer. Furthermore, using outsourced individuals could also present legal issues, financial setbacks, and provide limited control over outcomes. To try and mitigate the damages of outsourcing, you should use service level agreement (SLA) contracts with your vendors which ensure (with penalties) that you receive the desired performance and that expectations are met. Another disadvantage of outsourcing includes cultural differences. Outsourcing is often accomplished between organizations with different backgrounds, languages, and cultural differences. To outsource successfully, you should implement corporate policy that provides data security and protects the privacy of your customers. While cost reduction is a valuable benefit, you should be aware of outsource individuals who may have hidden costs associated with the work they provide.

# CHAPTER 12

# How You Lead Will Follow You

## EFFECTIVE LEADERSHIP

### TAXONOMY OF LEADERSHIP

By serving and supporting employees, you can create a positive and productive business environment. As a business owner, your leadership style plays a significant role in the success of your business and your employees' perceptions of the business. By satisfying employees through listening to their needs, adapting to their situations, creating a positive exchange, and building trust, you will have the support needed to create and innovate within your business which is helpful in motivating employees and generating positive customer relationships.

## ENTREPRENEURSHIP

The elements of entrepreneurship include an appetite for risk and the ability to spot opportunities. The propensity to take financial and career oriented risks are often attributed to entrepreneurs. However, while entrepreneurs generally take risk involving business opportunities, they must also be innovators and willing to continually take risks that challenge the status quo.

As a business owner, you must be both an entrepreneur and an innovator to remain relevant within your industry. An innovative entrepreneur is more likely to challenge assumptions due to what is known as creative intelligence which enables discovery by engaging both sides of the brain. While your entrepreneur side may know what decisions need to be made, the innovator in you understands how to make them work for a purpose. If you don't produce or motivate innovation within your business, you will eventually fall prey to businesses that do.

## MANAGEMENT

Managing your business effectively involves more than meaning well and supporting popular causes. The functions of being a manager are planning, organizing, leading, and controlling. As a manager, your role is to cope with complexity and bring a degree of order and consistency to the business at hand. Exhibiting leadership traits means not only influencing others but also doing so in a manner that enables your business to attain its goals.

Leadership and management are two distinctive, yet complementary, systems of action. Each has its own function and characteristics, and both are necessary for success in an increasingly complex and volatile business environment. Of course, not everyone can be good at both leading and managing.

Some people have the capacity to become excellent managers, but not strong leaders. Others have great leadership potential but have great difficulty becoming strong managers.

## LEADERSHIP

**Selling the Vision.** A vision is common in most major leadership theories and is defined in this context as an end-state or description of the future; an ideological goal that businesses, employees, and managers are morally satisfied in pursuing. Visions are generally focused on building innovation and creating change, and are considered to represent an idealized future state of what is desired. A vision is said to represent shared values and often has an ethical overtone. An effective vision is based on organizational purpose and must incorporate a goal. Many consider a vision paramount to building effective strategies and processes. Leaders with compelling visions can provide a sense of purpose and meaning to followers. A leaders' vision can affect the goals of a business considering that it affects the direction of action, the intensity of effort, and effort persistence.

## LEADERSHIP POWER

In recent years, the study of analyzing leadership power has increased. Fred C. Lunenburg said *"Power is* the ability to influence others." Power can be grouped into two categories: Organizational power (legitimate, reward, coercive) and personal power (expert and referent). Leadership power is defined as the possibility of inducing forces of a certain magnitude on another person. Naturally, leaders are considered an influencing agent of power over their followers.

As a leader in business, you are responsible for making certain that your employees achieve results and complete tasks as required. To produce the best possible results, you should exercise your leadership power and aim at making certain that employees are confident and comfortable, which involves making certain that there is trust and respect between you and your staff. The relationship between you and your employees should be one in which your workers trust you to make the right decisions. Healthy leadership provides stability and effective functioning for individuals and teams.

## TEAM LEADERSHIP

Nearly 80% of Fortune 500 companies use some form of team-based structures within their daily operations to help in organizing work.[25] Many employees are involved in teamwork as a part of their daily job duties and responsibilities. As a leader, you are responsible for broadening and elevating team members' goals as well as creating team confidence. You are also responsible for managing team conflicts, building relationships, engaging members, and taking responsibility for projects. Your leadership has a considerable impact on team members' attitudes toward their jobs, team climate, and performance. You should begin managing your team by setting a meeting with team members and have them introduce themselves to one another. This will allow members to build relationships and get to know one another on a personal level and in a comfortable setting.

As a leader, your role is to establish a team that can work efficiently to satisfy stakeholders, customers, and productivity. You should build your team based on their strengths and past performances. To prevent a power struggle within the group, where stronger members ignore the lower status individuals' suggestions and ideas, you should not only manage the needs of

[25] Magni, M., & Maruping, L. M. (2013). Sink or Swim: Empowering Leadership and Overload in Teams' Ability to Deal with the Unexpected. Human Resource Management, 52(5), 715-739. doi:10.1002/hrm.21561

the team, but also the individual members.

Within a team setting, team members should be able to react effectively to unanticipated, non-routine, and unstructured situations to achieve team objectives. To manage an effective team, the leader should create a structure that allows for open and efficient communication, shared responsibilities, and proper goal and time management. Additionally, sharing leadership tasks can help build trust and cooperation among team members. By sharing tasks, members gain strength, motivation, and encouragement.

**Virtual Teams.** Project teams are composed of individual team members who have varying viewpoints. This is heightened in virtual teams where members are from different locations and experience different cultures, beliefs, interests, distance, and standards. To keep up the morale of virtual team members, you should remain in touch on a regular basis and build rapport with team members. It would be your responsibility to motivate members via telephone calls and video conferencing which could help decrease member isolation. When working in a virtual team, culture and diversity can also affect how the team functions. Leaders interacting in diverse teams will be more susceptible to volatile relationships because of potential cultural misunderstandings. This is because diverse virtual team members can hold very different assumptions about mental modes and social interactions.

## LEADERSHIP STYLES

Effective leaders with vision have been shown to have a significant impact on followers' creativity, inspiration, achievement, team innovation, and organizational performance. Furthermore, vision and inspiration can promote positive organizational outcomes, change, and performance. With nearly 80% of companies using some form of team-based structure, creating a healthy team environment can be helpful in organizing work performance.

**Transformational leaders** may be best for motivating and appealing to followers' common ideals and ethical values. Transformational leaders use emotional cues and gestures to communicate their vision and build commitment. Leaders can better achieve their vision by engaging followers and creating a shared organizational vision with followers.

Transformational leaders seek to work with members to create a positive future that focuses on improving the status quo. Proper leadership is a key factor in organizational success. Transformational leaders focus on the higher needs of the company and use the full potential of workers by going beyond the social exchange. A transformational leader can have a great impact on the self-concept of employees by utilizing encouragement and intellectual stimulation. These types of leaders believe in building the capabilities of their followers and strive to enhance their knowledge and skills through regular feedback and building trust and respect.

An example of a transformational leader would be a principal at an educational facility. A principal has the task of overseeing the school's operation and making sure that the students are appropriately affected by his leadership decisions. To do this successfully, the principal must build the organization so that the teachers support the development and direction of its goals. This would require the principal to not focus directly on controlling or supervising curriculum, but to share the leadership role with those that have a direct impact on the students. This method is called controlling from above, and it stimulates change from the bottom-up.

**Transactional leaders** focus on maintaining the normal workflow of operations. These types of leaders will use disciplinary powers, awards, and an array of incentives to motivate employees to perform their best. Transactional leaders are focused on satisfying quotas on a day-to-day basis and additionally tend to go beyond the normal day-to-day routine and focus on creating a solid team of employees by promoting team building. Transactional leaders motivate their employees through setting goals, implementing incentives, and providing opportunities for personal and professional growth.

Transactional leadership is noted when a leader exchanges something of value with a follower. This exchange is based on the follower being credited for positive performance. The goal of this type of leadership is for both the leader and follower to enter into a mutually beneficial exchange in pursuit of a higher purpose.

**Situational leadership** is based on the theory that effective leadership requires an appropriate response based on rational understanding for each unique situation. A situational leadership style is classified as a contingency or behavioral model that centralizes the leader's behavior as task relevant and adaptive to the group concerned in a given situation. To establish a relationship between a situational leader and follower, key factors such as performance readiness of the follower must be determined. Situational leadership is a combination of three major features: Relational concerns, leader direction, and the motivational level of followers.

Situational leaders place attention on the functionality of the environment, such as maturity and follower psychological state. By focusing on the members' well-being, an effective relationship between the leader and follower is created. The relationship between the situational leader and the follower is considered to be an individualized concept under this type of model. A manager in a work environment who needs to accommodate a disabled employee is an example of a situational leader. As a leader, the manager must place a unique situational approach on the needs and functional capabilities between the disabled employee and the workplace. The leader must be fluid and willing to adjust for the needs of the disabled employee.

**Servant leadership** requires the ability to listen to the needs of others, having empathy, awareness, persuasion, stewardship, and a desire to work toward building a community within the organization. A servant leader behaves ethically and motivates followers without having ulterior motives to satisfy *their* personal desires. This type of leader prioritizes the needs of their followers and is more concerned about the success and well-being of others. Servant leaders are humble leaders who desire to stimulate strong relationships with their followers by encouragement. This servant approach creates a positive work environment and value for the organization.

Leaders who provide emotional support to followers working to reach their full potential can be seen as role models. A servant leader will seek to grow and transform their followers by providing guidance and direction for their followers.

**Authentic leadership** theorists propose that authentic leaders influence followers from a moral perspective. This type of influence is said to energize followers by creating meaning and constructing a positive reality.

There are four elements of self-awareness identified in an authentic leader: Values, cognitions regarding identity, emotions, and motives/goals. Authentic leadership constructs the importance of leaders' inner life instead of focusing on leadership as having or doing. It assumes that inner imaginations and spiritual identity are what guide and motivate the leaders' behavior. Growing evidence suggest that an authentic leader approach is effective for organizations. This type of leadership is desirable and considered to achieve positive outcomes. The term authenticity is described as "owning one's personal experiences."

If individuals know themselves, they will display higher levels of stability.

Persons who are not authentic are believed to be fragile, biased, and will have lowered self-esteem. Authentic behavior reflects consistency based on the leader's values, beliefs, and actions. Authentic leaders are considered expressive of their authentic self and are known to foster high-quality relationships while projecting their values and visions onto followers. The theory of authentic leadership is a result of writings on transformational leadership, which suggest that not all transformational leaders are genuine. Authentic leadership is additionally considered a transparent and ethical leader that is open to accept followers' input.

**Leader-member exchange** is defined as a relationship created through task behavior and relationship behavior. Leader-member exchange theory asserts that relationships between leaders and followers will likely motivate followers to commit to organizational and leader goals. This type of leadership is said to potentially elevate knowledge sharing between leader and follower. Leader-member exchange and knowledge sharing are considered to be positively linked with a creative work involvement. In business, employees tend to enjoy a leader-member exchange as a high-quality relationship considering this type of leadership allows employees to engage in open and creative work processes and encourages positive perceptions. A leader-member exchange relationship requires both the leader and follower to agree and accept shared goals that will fulfill a mutual interest. These relationships positively alter the impact of organizational outcomes.

**Mark Zuckerberg** is known to have a goal-oriented mindset and is fully focused on leading his team to produce the best social media platform in the world. Today, Mark Zuckerberg is the youngest billionaire on earth and Chairman/CEO of the world's most popular website, Facebook. At its headquarters in Menlo Park, California, each Friday Facebook holds a question and answer session for its employees and users. This forum is as open discussion where Zuckerberg is known for sharing his personal thoughts on the company's direction.

The Facebook work environment includes an on-site doctor, chiropractor, and physical therapist. In addition, the café at Facebook offers employees gourmet meals within a setting designed by a team that built a four-star hotel in New York. The building also includes vending machines stocked with computer accessories where users can swipe their identification card and get items such as a new computer charger, battery pack, or keyboard. Once a year, Facebook rents a local park and allows their entire office staff to play games such as dodgeball, kickball, and soccer. In the Facebook work environment, employee comfort and happiness is paramount. Facebook believes that if its employees are comfortable and happy then they will be more productive.

At Facebook, employees, are not assigned projects, but are allowed to choose the projects in which they are most interested. This method of leadership gives the employees power, courage, and the freedom to choose their path of success. Zuckerberg believes that great people who work with clear direction can produce positive results. He believes that employees should be hired based on their passion and not their skill-set. In an interview, he explained that, "skills can be taught, passion can't."

According to Yishan Wong, a former employee at Facebook, as a boss, Zuckerberg began as being cutthroat, and sometimes awkward. His leadership style eventually matured through the five years while Wong was employed with the company between 2005 and 2010. Wong explained that Zuckerberg expected debate, wasn't sentimental, and he pushed people beyond what they thought was possible of themselves. Wong further explained that in working for Facebook, you must be self-motivated, confident, emotionally secure, and willing to accept the challenges. To help with building his leadership style, Zuckerberg sought-out mentors who eventually helped him create a clear vision for his company. Andrew Bosworth, a current software engineer at Facebook, described Zuckerberg's leadership as fearless, tireless, and challenging, but with good reason. The results of his leadership expose unthinkable talent within the employees.

Implementing proper leadership is paramount for organizational success, considering leaders have a considerable impact on members' attitudes toward their job and their performance. In comparing leadership styles, transactional, transformational, and situational leaders can be very effective in creating a healthy organizational environment. While there is no one leadership style that works in every situation, in organizational teams, transformational leaders can be considered best suited for creating positive outcomes.

In developing healthy organizations, you should implement processes, programs, and interventions that will help produce effective leadership potential. Transformational, transactional, and situational leadership styles may help lead employees to trust your leadership which can generate and increase productivity. If you have an understanding of your leadership style, you can be mindful of your actions toward your employees. In understanding leadership styles, assessments can be helpful at improving your relationships with employees. Being informed of your leadership style can help gain insight into business problems and produce solutions for challenges that effect your overall business productivity, reputation, revenue, and customer loyalty.

# GLOSSARY

Made in the USA
Coppell, TX
11 February 2021